CW00394927

PICKING UP T

The Author *c* 1930

(Photo courtesy Margaret Walter)

PICKING UP THREADS

The Complete Reminiscences of a Bradford Mill Girl

By Maggie Newbery

Edited by James Ogden

BRADFORD LIBRARIES

First published 1993
by Bradford Libraries
Central Library
Prince's Way
Bradford
West Yorkshire
BD1 1NN

This work is an extended and revised version of *Reminiscences of a Bradford Mill Girl: autobiography of Maggie Newbery*, published by the Libraries Division, City of Bradford Metropolitan Council in 1980, and reprinted in 1980, 1981 and 1983.

© James Ogden 1992

All rights reserved

ISBN 0 907734 37 5

Printed by the Alden Press, Osney Mead, Oxford, OX2 0EF

CONTENTS

ILLUSTRATIONS

FOREWORD

"Whatever happened to Maggie?" is a question library staff have frequently been asked. Here is the answer!

The Reminiscences of a Bradford Mill Girl was one of the first books published by Bradford's library service and it proved to be so popular that it was printed three times and sold 9,500 copies. Now, long out-of-print and constantly requested, we are pleased to make Maggie's story available again. We have taken the opportunity to add some material which continues Maggie's reminiscences well beyond her mill-working days. We have also included some illustrations and generally up-graded the earlier booklet.

Maggie died in 1980 and our thanks go to her daughter, Margaret Walter, for permission to republish, and to her nephew, James Ogden, for editing the text and providing some family photographs. Thanks also to Carol Greenwood for help in finding some appropriate illustrations, and to David P. Pratt and Stroud Riley Drummonds for permission to use photographs.

In the last fifteen years Bradford Libraries have published some thirty books. The success of this publishing activity is immensely satisfying, and due in part to the success of *Reminiscences*; but this book is our first "second edition". I hope as many people enjoy this edition as enjoyed the first.

Bob Duckett
(Reference Librarian,
Bradford Libraries)
April 1993

INTRODUCTION

'Maggie is writing her memoirs' was the rumour that went round soon after my aunt reached the age of seventy. Undismayed by such satire, only to be expected in our family, she wrote most of this book in the next three years, and added the conclusion six years later. When I read the manuscript I soon saw that it should be published, though it needed some revision. As I typed it I put in standard punctuation and paragraphs, and left out personal details and repetitions. Maggie approved of these changes. Unfortunately I worked rather slowly, and before I had finished part of the book was published by Bradford Libraries as *Reminiscences of a Bradford Mill Girl*. That was in 1980, the year of Maggie's death; she lived to see her work in print, but not long enough to enjoy her success as an author; the book was reprinted three times and sold 9500 copies.

This second, complete edition of the *Reminiscences* comprises: the first seven chapters of the first edition, with minor corrections; chapter eight of the first edition, revised and divided into two chapters (eight and nine); four additional chapters; and the conclusion. The editorial principles remain the same. I think it can now be claimed that almost everything Maggie wrote has been included, and that almost everything is in her own words; there have been some changes in the order of sentences, to improve the narrative flow. Her daughter Margaret has approved of these alterations and has supplied the title *Picking up Threads*, which relates of course to the mill girl's craft, to Maggie's effort of memory, and less obviously to my aunt's attempts at holding together the scattered Lount family.

As was to be expected, there were enthusiastic reviews of the first edition in the *Telegraph & Argus*, the *Yorkshire Post*, and the *Yorkshire Evening Post*, emphasising the changes in working-class life between 1920 and 1980. 'Count your blessings', was one headline. But I was delighted to see a discerning review by Jill Liddington in the academic periodical *Oral History*.* She found the *Reminiscences* 'outstanding as a labour

---

* Spring 1982; vol. 10, no. 1, pp. 67–9. See also *Telegraph & Argus* 30 June 1980, 12 January and 10 August 1981, 13 October 1983; *Yorkshire Post* 31 July 1980; *Yorkshire Evening Post* 14 January 1981.

history text', and remarked on 'its sensitive portrayal of the traumatic change from childhood to adulthood pinpointed at the first day at work as a twelve year old half-timer'. Ms Liddington quoted from Chapter V and emphasised Maggie's mixed feelings:

> Threepence *was* a lot to spend, but she began to wonder at what cost it was acquired. Maggie's detailed description of mill life should certainly be a prescribed text for any historian wanting to understand Britain's once flourishing textile industry.

It only needs adding, I think, that the book as a whole tells the archetypal tale of a farming family uprooted from the land, forced to make the best of things in an industrial city. Maggie's week's holiday on her grandfather's farm at Weel, and her return to Bradford, is a poignant episode.

The complete edition makes it clearer that Maggie soon determined not to be a mill girl, and tried all alternatives. She was successively a domestic servant, an after-sales representative with Singer sewing machines, a probationer nurse at Menston Asylum, a waitress at Manningham Park café, and a baths attendant. Finally she found her vocation as a swimming teacher, and for some forty years between 1930 and 1970 she taught Bradfordians to swim and to save lives. These years coincide with her courtship and marriage to Stanley Newbery, of whom she says: 'Stan had been through the First World War and had seen such misery and suffering that all he now wished to do was bring a little happiness into the lives of all he came in contact with.' Now the spirits of that happy pair often sit on a seat at Crayke, enjoying the view of the great plain of York, drinking coffee from their thermos flask, and munching jam sandwiches made with currant teacakes.

As well as her *Reminiscences* Maggie wrote some poems and stories in Yorkshire dialect, two of which were published in the Yorkshire Dialect Society's *Summer Bulletin*: a short story, 'The Jumble Sale' (1974), and a poem on the view of Bradford from the top of Bolton Road, 'T'Valley Leets' (1987).

I would like to acknowledge help in preparing this book from: Mr David Neave, of the Hull University Adult Education Department; Miss Elvira Willmott, of the Bradford Libraries Local Studies Division; Mr Bob Duckett, of the Bradford Libraries Reference Service; Dr Donald Walter; Mrs Margaret Walter; and Dr. John Ogden.

James Ogden
University of Wales
Aberystwyth

THE LOUNT FAMILY

Herbert Hudson Lount (1866–1933) married Mary Jane Clark (1869–1949) at St Mary's, Beverley (1891). Children:

1. Isabella ("Bella") (1891–1958)
2. Elizabeth ("Lizzie" or "Bessie") (1894–1978) married Walter Wood. Children: Kathleen, Joan, Jeffrey.
3. George (1895–1961) married (1) May Greenwood, (2) Eveline Hawksworth.
4. Charlotte Annie ("Annie") (1897–1982) married (1) James Ernest Lount (cousin), (2) John Lount (cousin). Children by first marriage: Dorothy, Hilda, Gordon.
5. Mary Ellen ("Nellie") (1898–1919)
6. Charles Edward ("Charlie") (1900–92)
7. Maggie (1901–80) married Stanley Newbery (1896–1966) at Salem Church, Oak Lane, Bradford (1937). One child: Margaret.
8. Alice (1903–80) married Reginald Shepherd. Children: Stella, Donald, David.
9. James Ernest (1905–28)
10. Ethel ("Hetty") (1907–87) married William Ogden. Children: James, John, Janet.
11. Harriet Lillian (1908–92) married Clarence Nicholson.
12. Harry (1910–) married Catherine Jenkinson.

Chapter 1

Crayke

I suppose I had better begin at the beginning. I was born at Norwood, Beverley, Yorkshire, on 20 April 1901. I was the seventh child of Mary Jane Clark and Herbert Hudson Lount, who were married at St Mary's, Beverley, on 8 April 1891. Before my arrival there were already Isabella (called Bella), Elizabeth (Lizzie, now better known as Bessie), George Herbert (George), Charlotte Annie (Annie), Mary Ellen (Nellie), and Charles Edward (Charlie). My mother told me that when she was discussing with my father what I was to be named my father said, "Well, christen this one what you intend to call her", so I got Maggie - not Margaret but just plain Maggie.

We were poor, and I mean poor; my father was a farm labourer. He worked for his father, who had a farm at Weel, near Beverley. His wages were eighteen shillings a week. For a period my grandfather had a contract with Beverley Corporation for emptying earth middens. The closets in the town were simply boards with holes in, which adjoined the middens. All the filth and dirt was scraped out and shovelled on to the muck carts, to be carted away and used as manure. The stink must have been terrible, so the middens were emptied in the early morning (4 a.m. to 6 a.m.), and afterwards the women turned out and swilled all the remaining dirt away. However, there wasn't much money in farming in those days, so the money derived from this contract helped to get the farm going.

When I was expected my mother was busy decorating the bedroom. I must have been eager to make my début, as my mother had to go to bed while only half the room was papered. The doctor was sent for; a neighbour came in and prepared the bed by fixing a roller towel to the bed rail to assist my mother in labour. Hot water was supplied, and a few hours later I had arrived. Most babies were breast fed in those days, often for eighteen months and longer; baby foods were unknown and the only alternative was a wet nurse, but only the wealthy could afford them. However we all seemed to thrive, and in due course I was

Water Hall Farm, Crayke, 1992. (Photo courtesy James Ogden)

running about with my brothers and sisters, the older ones taking care of the younger ones.

Soon after I was born my father ceased to work for his father and started as a hay and straw dealer in his own right. Before I was two years old I was no longer the baby; my sister Alice was born on 27 January 1903. When I was nearly three my father, having lived sparingly and saved carefully, took Water Hall Farm, Crayke, and we moved there to take the tenancy on 1 April 1904. The first thing I remember about Water Hall Farm was that my brothers and sisters, whose ages ranged from ten to four (my eldest sister was now working), found that by opening an outhouse door we could make a full circuit of the house; which we did, and continued to run round and round the house, shouting and singing - very distracting to our parents who were trying to get everything into place. After a while I found I was the only one going round; everyone else had been found jobs to do.

The days at Crayke must have been happy ones. My mother always seemed busy; there were chickens and hens to feed, butter to make, and meals to prepare. I remember feeling a blank when my brother Charles started school. Then when I was five I started school. I had been well drilled beforehand on how to behave, and every sentence seemed to end with "or else you will get the cane". We lived about one mile away from the village. There was very little traffic on the roads in those days, just the odd farm cart or rully. The roads were very dusty, but there were plenty of distractions: the first primrose and violet to be found in the hedge bottoms, sometimes a bird's nest in the hedge. With the result that the last lap was usually made at a run, and as the school was at the top of a steep hill we generally arrived breathless. Because we had such a long way to travel we were allowed to sit in the school and eat our sandwiches at lunchtime; then we could either go for a walk in the village or sit in school and read.

I remember my first day because I disgraced myself. I suppose the day must have seemed very long, and during the afternoon I started crying and saying I wanted to go home. My older sister Lizzie was sent for and told to take me home, as the teacher could do nothing with me. Lizzie was not at all pleased; I was made to feel that I had let the family down and was just a great baby. Our head teacher was Mr. Watson, and it pleased us to talk of him as a very hard man. We had a little jingle we used to sing, but not in his hearing. It went like this:

> Old Mr Watson is a good old man;
> He tries to teach us all he can,
> Reading, writing, and arithmetic,
> But he never forgets to use the stick.
>
> When he starts, he makes us dance
> Out of England into France,
> Out of France into Spain,
> Over the hills and home again.

I continued at school without any further mishap. My brothers and sisters were kept busy on the farm. The only job allotted to me, that I remember, was the collecting of kindling. As was usual at this time we had a large kindling stack in the yard. Any member of the family who came across some useful firewood while out walking was expected to bring it home and throw it on the stack. My brother and I had to go each evening and collect enough to light two fires next morning.

Water Hall Farm was like most farms at this time: in a state of very poor repair. The house itself was warm and comfortable and not too large. I have heard my mother say it was the most happy time of her life. My father worked the farm well and we prospered. It was here on 1 January 1905 that my brother James Ernest was born, and on 24 January 1907 my sister Ethel was born, making the family ten. I also met my eldest sister Bella here for the first time that I remember. She had been in service. My mother, who had an accident while shooing chickens away from the kitchen door, was temporarily lame, and my sister came home to help. I remember thinking how grown up she was (she would be fifteen), and how clever she was because she made a little jingle about my mother's accident and we all used to chant it:

My mother's got the habit of kicking;
One day she let fly at a chicken;
The chicken did die;
She put it in a pie;
And the bones didn't take much picking.

I don't remember much more of the time we spent at Crayke, except that at Easter everyone went to Bransby Hill to roll their Easter eggs. These eggs were dyed different colours through boiling in herbs and had our names on; they were really very artistic. We would all go to the top of the hill, which was a grassy bank, and roll our eggs; if they managed to reach the bottom intact, we believed we should be very lucky during the next year. However most of them managed to hit a stone and get cracked, when they were speedily peeled and eaten. I suppose really it was a social occasion; our mothers sat at the top of the hill and talked, while we chased the eggs, hoping our mothers had brought a few spares.

Chapter 2

Nun Monkton

It was in April 1907 that we left Crayke and went to live at Poole Bridge Farm, Nun Monkton. This was a bigger farm. The house was set back from the road the length of a small paddock. The house itself was large and roomy. There was a back kitchen where the men left their dirty boots and wet clothing. Here was a kitchen range, and usually there was a fire in the grate, a fender in front of the fire, and a tabbed rug on the floor. Just inside the door there was a table on which stood a bowl and jug, soap, and a flannel; the pump was in the yard outside. The men of course were early risers. They would get a bowl of water and wash before breakfast, but they invariably left the dirty water in the bowl. We children were then sent into the kitchen to wash, and if we weren't caught out we would use the already dirty soapy water rather than go and pump some more. On cold winter mornings the used water always felt so much warmer. When everyone was ready we went through to the front kitchen, where there was a long table down one side, and forms to sit on. My father sat at the head, then the men (we never had more than two, usually one), then we children took our places at either side. My mother usually sat at the other end. My father used to say grace, but eventually this seemed to lapse and we each said our own as soon as we sat down. Breakfast consisted chiefly of cold boiled bacon and bread for the men, but we children always had a bowl of bread and milk, that is, a thick slice of bread cut into small squares and covered with boiling milk. Sometimes this was followed by a piece of fruit pie or half a slice of bread and jam.

This kitchen always smelt warm and clean. There was a large kitchen range on one side that was polished with black lead until it shone. In front of this was a hearthstone, which my mother kept white by washing and smearing over with whitening. On this rested the fender, which reflected the glow of the fire, and caused my mother hours of work keeping it polished. The walls of the kitchen were white. They were lime washed about four times a year to keep the flies away. There were no insecticides

Pool Bridge Farm, Nun Monkton, 1992. (Photo courtesy James Ogden)

in those days, and the only fly catcher I ever saw before leaving Pool Bridge was a kind of bottle where the flies were attracted by the smell of beer or vinegar, entered the bottle, were unable to get out, and so were drowned. At the end of the room stood the flour bin, shaped like a desk. The lid was lifted and flour from five or ten stone bags was emptied into the bin, which was never allowed to get empty. Except for a wooden armchair which was usually at the head of the table, and a rocking chair, this comprised the whole of the furniture. The floor was red brick, and was scrubbed once a week. On one wall hung a huge map of Yorkshire, which we were allowed to look at but not touch. It fascinated me to think that besides Kirk Hammerton and Nun Monkton, which I knew, there were all these other places which I didn't know. When the church magazine arrived I used to love to find on the map any of the other places mentioned in it. I felt it was really something to have read about them and to know they were there on the map.

Through the kitchen we entered 'the room', which was only used on Sundays. Here we had a dresser with glass knobs on the drawers, and on it a few photographs and ornaments. There was a horse hair sofa on the side by the window, a square table in the centre of the room, two horse hair easy chairs, one at each side of the fireplace, and four upright chairs in polished mahogany. There were oil paintings of Disraeli,

Gladstone and Cobden. Their eyes seemed to be always watching you. There was an iron fender and of course a tabbed rug.

From this room you entered the 'far' or 'best' room, which always smelt musty because no one ever went in except to dust it. Here was a carpet on the floor with a rather smaller tabbed rug in front of the fireplace. Here was our pride, a horse hair suite: sofa, two easy chairs, and four others. The covering used to rub your bare legs and was most uncomfortable, but as it looked nice and was I suppose a kind of status symbol, nobody minded. In the centre of the room was a round card table, on which was placed the family Bible and a most beautiful photograph album. There was a huge picture on the wall of Moses viewing the Promised Land. The colours were really lovely, but the rod he carried seemed to point accusingly at me. There was also a very nice china cabinet and a small desk.

There was another room, to the right of the front door as you entered, which was never furnished. We used to call it our playroom, and sometimes left in it a few boxes or anything else we found and treasured. The floor was red brick, and acted as a board to chalk on. We spent quite a lot of time here on rainy days. There were two staircases. One led up from the back kitchen to the boys' room. This was a huge room with three double beds in. The front stairs were directly opposite the front door. There were four bedrooms. The one over the playroom was known as the guest room and was not used very often. It was in this room that my sister Harriet Lillian was born, and later my brother Harry.

Our bedroom was at the end of the house. We had a bed on the floor; a straw mattress with a feather bed on the top. As there were four of us sleeping together we slept the wrong way on the bed and our feet were often peeping out, but we were always warm and comfortable. The only other furniture was a blanket box. We used to decorate this box with our ornaments, such as bits of broken pot we found while digging in the garden, and tea packets. My two older sisters Annie and Nellie had the other bedroom. It had a bed and a chest of drawers with a swing looking glass, which was draped with a piece of curtain. I thought this was very nice. There was also a square of carpet on the floor, and I used to wonder if when we got a bit older Alice and I would have this room, as by that time my older sisters would be in service. We all grew up expecting to go into service when we were fourteen.

There were of course two pantries leading from the kitchen. These were quite roomy and had wide shelves on three sides. The closet or privy was at the back of the house and quite some distance away, no doubt on account of the smell. It was a double one, that is to say there were two holes in one

Old School, Kirk Hammerton, 1992. Now a private house. (Photo courtesy James Ogden)

long seat, so you could if so inclined sit and hold a conversation while doing the needful; and this we children often did. It's surprising how many confidences were given and received here. I remember also we all had a preference for one seat, so if two of us were going together we would shout "foggy for the one with the lid on", and if you got your claim in first it was undisputed. Why we used the word "foggy" to stake a claim I don't know, but all the children in the village did. I never heard the word used in the West Riding of Yorkshire, but it was used extensively in the East Riding.

Although the farm was in the parish of Nun Monkton we went to Kirk Hammerton school. My father took us the first time. We all climbed into the trap and off we went. It was of course a church school and when we arrived the vicar was paying one of his calls. My father led us in, and went and had a word with the vicar and the headmaster. Before long he came back and told us to get back into the trap, as the vicar refused to let us stay, because we were not in his parish. My father refused to let us go to Nun Monkton, as it was over three miles away and Kirk Hammerton was just a little nearer, so while the powers-that-be made up their minds he was summoned for keeping us away from school, and had to appear at Knaresborough court. We enjoyed five weeks holiday, and would have been quite content had the wrangling lasted five months. We were finally given permission to attend Kirk Hammerton school.

I would be six years of age when I started. No one seemed to think almost three miles was a long way to walk for a child of that age, and I was certainly pleased to go. It was fun wandering along the lanes, and unless we tied up with another family who came from Skip Bridge we rarely met anyone. My mother used to see that we set off in good time with sandwiches for dinner, and reminded us that when the 8.50 express to York was seen we should be near Kirk Hammerton station or we should be late. In winter she used to fill a large can with broth or soup, which she heated so we were able to warm our hands on the can. Our teacher, Miss Bailey, would stand this can on the stove in the centre of the room, and heat it up again for our dinner. Sometimes there would be another can from the Skip Bridge contingent, and the aromas from these were most tantalising to hungry children trying to grapple with the Three Rs.

There would be about 50 to 60 children attending the school, and these would be of all ages from five to fourteen. I liked school. Miss Antony, who took the younger children, was very kind; so was Miss Bailey, but she was able to convey the message that we were there to work. I suppose she was a dedicated teacher, but even the big boys had a healthy respect for her, and knew better than to be cheeky when Miss Bailey was about. At that time a lot of our lessons were done on slate by pencil, a most laborious way of writing or drawing. Miss Bailey was not above using the cane when necessary, but her usual form of punishment was to give lines, 100 or 500 according to the degree of crime. The lines were always one of two: either, "Manners make the man", or, "Politeness goes a long way and does not cost anything." Needless to say while waiting for the verdict we hoped for the former. Unless Miss Bailey told us to rub the lines out immediately we hid them to be used another time. We once found her cane while we were roaming around after dinner, and put it in the stove. However she found another and we knew better than to touch anything of hers when she had finished with us.

About once a month the vicar would call in and examine us. I didn't like the vicar. He was very stern, and I was afraid of him and always conscious of my ink-stained fingers and untidy hair, which my brothers would call rat tails. The vicar did not like us either. He had not wanted us, feeling that we ought to have gone to Nun Monkton; and to aggravate matters my mother, after sending us to church the first six months or so, allowed us to leave and go to the Wesleyan Chapel, and as we swelled the ranks of the Wesleyans the church ranks were depleted. We really enjoyed going to

Sunday School. The hymns which take me back there are: "There is a green hill far away", "All things bright and beautiful", "Onward Christian soldiers", and "Tell me the old old story". We also learnt poems and songs: "Sweet and low", "Robin Adair", "Hiawatha", "We are seven", and "The Brook". If we got a bit lively the teacher would land us one with his Bible, one way of hammering in the good word I suppose.

There was another thing that annoyed me about the vicar; he demanded a curtsey. When he entered the school we all stood to attention, and before sitting down the girls curtsied and the boys touched their forelocks; I thought the boys had the best of it. If we encountered him outside we must also curtsey. Now the funny thing is that really as a little girl I loved curtseying, but not to the vicar. If we caught sight of him outside and thought he hadn't seen us, we would immediately become very interested in something in the hedge bottom or pretend our boot laces wanted attention, and our heads would be down till we thought it safe to look up—sometimes to find the vicar standing only a few yards away regarding us as miserable offenders. We would then colour up and bob a curtsey. I don't suppose it did us any harm, but it did not engender love of the church. Now the chapel was different; we sang hymns with choruses that we could really let ourselves go in, and the teacher presented the Bible to us in the form of stories, which of course we liked.

For school we always wore boots which came just over the ankles. These had to be cleaned every evening. We had to use blacking which came in packets and was put in an old saucer or tin. To make it pliable we would add a drop of water or tea or spit, and then brush it on our boots. With a softer brush we polished until the boots really shone and our arms ached. We just knew we couldn't get away with anything but really bright boots for school.

The Band of Hope movement was very strong at this time, and as good Methodists we all signed the pledge. We were given a certificate and a piece of blue ribbon to wear in our coats; we were known as the Blue Ribbon Brigade. We also had Temperance Sunday, when all we children got up and recited poems about the harmful effects of strong drink. It was quite usual to see members of the congregation with tears streaming down their faces vowing they would never drink again and signing the pledge on their way out. Alas too many of them forgot and would turn up again the next year and sign again. Some of the pieces were most harrowing; I remember one my sister said once, and I always felt so sorry for her while she was saying it, because to me it sounded so real:

My Story

I want to tell you my story,
  Because I have suffered so
Through the drink which today is causing
  Such misery, sin, and woe.

I was married quite young to a man who was loved
  And honoured by all who knew him;
And I knew my life would happy be,
  When gladly I yielded it to him.

I can't tell how happy we were the first years,
  When two little children were given;
We both tried to make our home happy on earth,
  And prepare for a better in heaven.

But soon I was stricken with fever,
  And many despaired of my life;
And oft I saw Harry with tears in his eyes
  Kneeling down to pray for his wife.

God heard those prayers that were offered;
  He raised me once more from my bed;
But Oh in the years that have followed,
  How I wish I had died then instead.

For when I had thus far recovered,
  The doctor, he ordered me wine,
And sometimes a little brandy,
  And port from time to time.

With reluctance I followed his orders;
  But I took it and loved it too,
And soon the reluctance all vanished,
  I took it but secretly though.

At last I threw all shame aside;
  I drank from morn till eve;
I felt that if I did not drink,
  I surely should not live.

And once when I had been drinking
  Right on for a week or more,
I saw a sight that startled me,
  As I entered our cottage door.

Our youngest babe, our darling,
  Was lying with fevered brow,
His little lips all parched and dry;
  I think I see him now.

And as the door I entered
  He held up his tiny hands

And begged for a drink of water,
  But alas I could not stand.

I went into the kitchen
  And sank into a chair
And strangers came to tend him
  While his mother sat sleeping there.

But alas when I awoke
  A waxen figure lay -
A sunbeam lighting up his face,
  The first of coming day.

And now I have finished my story,
  And I trust it will a warning be:
If any here love the wine cup,
  Give it up, friends, tonight, and be free.

Another highlight in our year was the Sunday School Treat, which came somewhere around Whitsuntide. A field was set aside and there were races for every age. I still have a china mug I won at Kirk Hammerton. Tea was served outside, weather permitting, and we were allowed to stuff ourselves. There were seats around the field, where the older people could sit and talk. There was always a tug of war for the older boys, and the sports were usually concluded with a cricket match.

Another great day was the Christmas Tea, which was served in the schoolroom. We played all the usual games, usually had a Christmas cracker, and finished up with a present, an orange and a few sweets. I remember getting a doll's carriage once. It was made of cane and had three wheels, one at the front and two at the back, like an invalid chair. I never remember having a doll to put in, but I dressed a peg up and made a doll of that. I also wheeled about any cats or kittens I could get hold of. When you haven't much you learn how to improvise, and no doubt I got just as much pleasure out of these things as I would have done out of the most expensive doll. When playing shops at home we had quite a lot to stock with: a turnip was peeled and cut into cubes and became bread, potatoes peeled and sliced became bacon, carrots made teacakes.

There was only one store at Kirk Hammerton, and it was here that we brought our halfpennies. We usually had a halfpenny to share between the two of us about twice a week, so we were not overloaded with sweets. As sweets were about 4 ounces for a penny, 2 ounces between two of us was quite something, and we often got six or more sweets each. Licorice comfits and aniseed balls were the favourites, aniseed balls being 20 for a halfpenny.

We had a large orchard, so in the autumn we had plenty of apples. They were mostly Keswicks, but one tree we called the Painted Lady. The apples had beautiful red stripes and tasted wonderful. My mother used to store these for eating in the winter. We had a swing attached to this tree, and we would swing for hours hoping to shake some of the apples down. In the summer we would go brambling. There were loads of blackberries in the hedges. When gathering them for jam we would go with a pail, and would often come home with two pailfuls. My mother would then have a jamming day, and the larder would be stocked for winter. We also gathered hazel nuts, and quite a lot of crab apples, which made delicious jelly.

In those days no one ever thought of going away for holidays. Holidays for children were a time of taking lunch down to the workers in the field, and when the corn was being cut off following behind the reaper and stooking the corn; and there were always jobs to be found on the farm for anyone who looked bored. Haymaking was the most fun. We would be given a hay fork and told to go turn the hay. This generally finished with us throwing the hay all over each other and rolling in it. When they were leading the hay we would help by gathering the hay together making haycocks; these were then forked onto the rully, and when it was piled high one of the men would sometimes lift us to the top, and we would ride home feeling like lords of all we surveyed. The threshing time was most exciting. The threshing machine was hired, and would arrive early one morning; men were borrowed from neighbouring farms. The corn was fed into the machine, and by a process which seemed to me magic the straw was ejected and the corn run through little funnels into sacks, which when full were tied up, removed, and another quickly put into place. No time was wasted as no one wanted to employ the threshing machine longer than necessary; as my father would have said, "It's all money".

The River Nidd flowed through one of our fields, and occasionally we would have a picnic on the river bank. My mother would sometimes join us. There would be a large basket full of cheese or jam sandwiches, lots of pastries and cakes, and usually a packet of sweets. I think they called them "Lovers' Whispers". They had little mottoes on them such as "I love you", "You are my heart's delight", and "Be my honey bee", and we had lots of fun reading these. On hot days we would take our shoes and stockings off, and paddle on the river's edge. There was a branch of a tree that went well over the river; we would climb onto this, and were quite sure that if we fell into the water we would be able to swim out. I have lived long enough to know that we would probably have drowned, but at that time all the world was ours and we had no fears.

I remember one rather frightening experience. We had gone down with my father and one of the men to hoe turnips. This is a rather boring and back-aching job of pulling out lots of the seedlings and leaving one in about every eight inches. I soon got tired and was told to go sit on the bank at the side of the field and look after my younger brother, Jim, who would be about two years old. Well, we had gathered flowers and were sitting on the bank playing with them. It was a very hot sultry afternoon, and we were lying in the long grass on the bank when I became aware of a different noise—it wasn't the insects. I sat up quickly and looked behind me. There just by a bush was an adder, I would say sitting up looking at us. I had never seen one before, though I had heard about them. However, I didn't hesitate a moment; I grabbed Jim's hand and said "run", and we ran out of that field and across the next, home. I did of course relate what I had seen, but nobody paid much attention. Adders had been seen in that district, but so rarely that it was hardly believable. However, the following night the man went into the stable to feed the horses; he put his hand in the corn bin, and scooped up the adder, which was curled asleep. He was so scared he just flung it, and it landed on the muck heap outside. My father, who had been near at hand when he heard the man shout, was outside with a hay fork, with which he stabbed the adder just below the head. This had a rather quieting effect on our picnics, and when we went out for walks we always had a look for adders before sitting down. My father did come across another in the big meadow. He killed it, again by stabbing it with a hay fork. It was a very big one, over a yard long, and the markings of green and black were really lovely; one side was silver and looked lovely in the afternoon sun. It finished up on the scrap heap and all the locals said we shouldn't be bothered any more now. After hearing about the first one they had all predicted another would come to its funeral. My father set fire to them on the muck heap. When we told Miss Bailey about the second one she said it was a pity it had been destroyed; it should have been sent to York or Knaresborough Museum.

We played all the usual games. It was surprising where the whips and tops came from as soon as the snow and cold weather had passed. We coloured the tops of our tops with crayons, so they looked pretty when spinning. Marbles, or "Taws" as it was more often called, was a great game among the boys, and almost every boy had his jealously guarded bag of taws. The girls would get the skipping rope out. Then the chants began as each girl went in to skip.

Little fat doctor, how's your wife?
Very well thankyou, that's allright;
Can't eat a bit of fish,
Or a bit of licorice,
O-U-T spells out.

A house to let, enquire within:
When I walk out, someone else walks in.

My mother said, I never should
Play with the gipsies in the wood;
If I did, she would say,
Naughty girl to disobey,
Disobey, disobey,
Naughty girl to disobey.

I have a bonnet, trimmed with blue.
Do you wear it? Yes, I do,
When I go to meet my John,
Then I put my bonnet on.

Ipsy gipsy lived in a tent;
She couldn't afford to pay the rent;
When the rent man came next day,
Ipsy gipsy ran away.

Lady, lady, touch the ground;
Lady, lady, turn right round;
Lady, lady, show your boot;
Lady, lady, take your hook.

All in together,
This fine weather;
I saw Peter,
Looking through the window,
O-U-T spells out.

Miss Bailey would have the men bring the Maypole out and erect it in the school yard, and we would dance round, plaiting the ribbons as we danced. I thought this was a huge Maypole, but actually it wasn't anything near so big as the one at Nun Monkton.

We played the usual ball games. There was one that I never saw played in Bradford. All the players (not more than seven) were given a day of the week. Then the starter would throw the ball up in the air, calling "Up for Monday!" or Tuesday or the day of her choice, who would then try to catch the ball before it hit the ground, the other players all running away from the "homey" as far as they could. If the girl managed to catch the ball before it hit the ground she would immediately throw it up again for someone else. If she missed it, she had to recover it, and call "Stop!" Everyone stood still, and she had to aim and hit someone with the ball. Then they were "out", everyone went back to the homey, and the game

continued. If her aim was poor, then she became the starter, and the game
continued with nobody out.

Our game of hopscotch varied to the one we played in Bradford. At
Kirk Hammerton we drew four triangles:

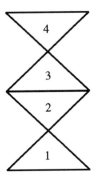

The first triangle we hopped into. Then we were allowed to rest with one
foot at each side of the point. Then hop, hop, rest, hop, turn and rest, and
the same back. This had to be done without touching any line. The next
time round was hop in the triangle, out, in, in, out, in, turn, come back
down the other side. Then the same was done, but now you selected a
nice flat piece of pot or stone, and as you hopped this was pushed into
the next triangle with your toe, if it rested on a line you were out. This
game was played by two, and when you were out your opponent took
her turn, and you each started where you left off. That is, first you did
the hopping and resting, then the hopping all the way, then hopping
and pushing the stone. If you were successful in getting it round you
next threw it into the second triangle, then three, then four, and the first
to reach this was the winner. Now in Bradford we had a different square:

5	4
6	3
7	2
8	1

We hopped all round the first time, then started with the stone, hopping and pushing it with our toes till we reached No. 8, and whoever got there first was the winner.

We had great fun at voting time. We didn't know what it was all about, of course, but we did know you either favoured Blue or Yellow. Most of us favoured Blue, just because it was blue. We would find a piece of blue ribbon and pin it on our dress. We then ran around shouting:

> Blue for ivver!
> Yellow's gone doon river
> With a fork in its guts
> And a knife in its liver!
> Blue for ivver!

We would then chase anyone who dared show a yellow ribbon.

We always remembered 29 May as Oak Apple Day, and we would not have dared to go to school without a sprig of oak, preferably with the apple on, pinned to our clothes. We also took a few nettles with us, and anyone who had not got a sprig of oak was well and truly nettled. We chanted this rhyme:

> The twenty-ninth of May
> Is Oak Apple Day;
> If you don't give us a holiday
> We'll all run away.

Saturday night was bath night. The boiler in the kitchen was filled with water, the fire lit underneath, and when the water was on the boiling point the tub was brought out and bathing commenced. The tub was the one used for washing clothes. It was a wooden one, about a yard long, about 14 inches wide at the bottom, and wider at the top. It was placed on a clean bag on the kitchen floor and was about half filled with water. Soap powder was put in, and then the first one got in and was scrubbed from head to toe. A lading can full of water was poured over your head to rinse away the soap suds. Then out you came and got a good towelling, put your nightdress on, and went into the front kitchen and sat on the rug while your hair dried. The next one was now in the tub. The water was kept warm by taking a lading can full out, and adding one from the boiler. There were usually five or six of us for bathing. The room got nice and hot and steamy, our faces all shone from rubbing with the yellow soap, and we felt really clean. The last one out, the bath was emptied; usually one of the men would do this by swilling the yard outside. As our hair got dry my mother would plait it. Finally we had a drink of milk and went to bed.

Before the bathing started we all had our heads seen to. In order to keep nits and head lice away we were all given a good brushing in paraffin. Our heads were brushed over a newspaper so that any lice could be dealt with; we were then given a good combing with a small tooth comb. It all sounds very primitive now, but we kept free of head lice through my mother's determination that none of her children should be called lousy.

Occasionally as we were going to school we saw motor cars. They would be on the York-Knaresborough road, which was not tarmacadamed in those days, so on dry days they sent clouds of dust up, and we would shout after them, "Come and clean your stink up!" Not that they heard, but it pleased us. I was told they could do 10 miles an hour, which was almost unbelievable.

I remember my brother Charles telling us, after he had been with my father to York, that he had been in a room and a man had lit a lamp that hung from the ceiling by pressing a button near the door. This sounded fantastic and we just couldn't believe it. He stuck to his tale and said they were electric. Our parents were called in to settle the matter, while we wondered at the marvels of science. The only lighting arrangements we had seen were candles and lamps. I don't remember having any lighting arrangements for going to bed.

The moon generally gave sufficient light. It was considered far too dangerous for us to take a candle upstairs. The paraffin lamps were really warm and friendly; ours had a large globe and gave a good light. On winter nights it was trimmed long before darkness came; then when necessary it was lit and stood on the table. We sat up to the table if we wanted to read, sew, knit, or play games such as Ludo, Draughts and Snakes and Ladders.

Chapter 3

The Move to Bradford

I think all us children enjoyed living at Kirk Hammerton. But things were not going so well with our parents. We had a bad harvest. Then we started to lose cattle; there was an outbreak of foot and mouth disease. My father, who had struggled on for a year trying to recover from the bad harvest, tried to find consolation at the "Station Hotel", and now all too often when we came home from school we would see our trap standing outside the hotel. At this time there was no compensation for loss of cattle through foot and mouth disease, and as it spread we lost all our cattle and had no financial backing.

At this time we only had one man working for us, and he stayed on till the end. We never knew him by any other name but Ben. He came to us a tramp, asking for a job and a night's lodging in the barn. My mother asked him to saw some logs, gave him a meal, and told him he was welcome to sleep in the barn. The following morning she took him a bowl of bread and milk, and found him sitting in the straw delousing his shirt. She took one look at it and told him to throw it on the muck heap and burn it. She found him an old one of my father's. He was a good worker and a kind man. He always found time to listen to our troubles, and would carve us boats out of bits of wood, which we sailed on the slap holes, as we called puddles. He must have been with us about eighteen months, and I suppose when we left he would go on the road again unless he found another place.

Things certainly got worse with us, and I suppose we were caught up in the Industrial Revolution. Our parents decided to give up farming and live in Bradford, where with a large family like ours the children could work in the mills. At least we would be fed, and if some of the stories we heard were true our fortune would soon be made. We went bankrupt. The bailiffs were sent in, and these two men never left the house. Then came the day of the sale. First the farm implements were brought to the front of the house, and put out in the paddock for inspection. Then the furniture—the front room horsehair suite, the desk, and various other things. It was exciting to us children, but I remember slipping into the room, just to see what was left, and seeing my mother sitting there weeping; she had the baby, Harry, on her knee. I wanted to cry too; somehow the thought of going to Bradford lost its appeal. The day came to an end and most of the things outside had been sold. We were given some bread and milk and sent to bed. Soon after this my father and my brother Charles loaded what furniture we had onto a cart and took it to Bradford. My father had already got us a house and himself a job, and we followed on by train the following day. I went all round the house into every room to say goodbye to it. We had been out in the fields to gather primroses and violets to bring with us. I think a neighbour called and took us to the station. We got in the train and left Kirk Hammerton; now we were going to get rich in Bradford.

It was dark when we arrived there. The station seemed a huge bustling place. Mother was carrying the baby; Nellie, Alice and Jim were helping her with the luggage. She told me to keep tight hold of Hetty and Lillian's hands and follow them. We were met outside by my father, who guided us to where the Great Horton trams started. We got on, mother and father and seven children, and asked for tickets to Arctic Parade. The conductor was very cheerful and joked with us. When my father asked for two and seven halfs (children under 14 went half fare) he said, "Are all these yours?" My father replied, "Yes". He said, "And you're just coming; well, have a free ride just for luck", and he didn't take our fares. The seats were in twos and looked towards the front of the tram. I was very intrigued to know how it was propelled. I was sure there were no horses; I had looked as we got on. Now it was moving, not like a train but with a good deal of clanging. It was quite dark but I tried to look out at the front; I knew there was a driver there, but how did he make it go? At last we arrived at Arctic Parade and walked down to Livingstone Street, No. 36.

These houses were commonly known as back-to-back houses. That is, blocks of four, two facing south, two facing north, with their backs together, and joined onto the next four by a passage running under the bedroom. We had one room downstairs and two bedrooms. My father and Charlie had got some beds up, but we children slept on a mattress on the floor that night. How my mother and father coped is one of the wonders I shall never understand; but cope they did. Beds were put up, bedrooms divided by counterpanes acting as curtains, and some sort of order was maintained. A new life started for us. To children anything new is exciting, and this was all new. First, when we wanted a light we didn't need to trim the lamp. Now there was something called gas in the middle of the room coming down from the ceiling. You put a mantle on, turned a tap at the side, and there was a curious hissing sound. You then applied a lighted match, and you got a bang, splutter or flare which settled down to a steady clear glow lighting all the room. This was wonderful, almost like the electricity we had heard about. When you finished with the light you just turned it off and it went plop. We had brought the lamp with us but now we shouldn't need it. And we didn't need to go outside and pump water. There was a sink near the window, and if you wanted water all you needed to do was turn the tap. You could turn it more and more, and the water came faster and faster till it hit the stone sink with such a force that it splashed everything around. It was surprising what thirst we got and how fond we became of washing our hands. This was really the height of luxury: to have water without going outside and pumping. Then there was the closet or privy—but it was a privy no longer, it was a closet, and we only had to run down the passage and the second one was ours. After use we only had to pull a chain; a rush of water came and there it was, all clean again. You couldn't really call such a place a closet; we soon found from talking with our neighbours that it was a W.C. It was here that we ran into trouble. We had never had any neighbours, so it was hard to realise that the door at the back of our house was really someone else's home. After going to the W.C. we would run in by the back door as we thought, only to find ourselves in the wrong house.

After a time we got used to these things. My father had settled down and was working as a carter for one of the mills. He was with horses and liked the work. He realised there was no money for the public house and stayed at home in the evening. It was then that we missed the farm. One room and ten of us in it, my father trying to rest by the fireside while we laughed, quarrelled or sang as the mood took us. No wonder my mother would say, when it was fine, "Now off you go out and play", and we would play in the street till bedtime. Even so we were terribly over-crowded, and always looking out for a bigger house within our means.

We were sent to The Bell School on Southfield Lane. It was here that we found there were two sorts of Yorkshire. When I said I was "gan yam" (going home) it didn't mean a thing to the children I played with, and when one of them asked me if I would go out and "laik" (play) I thought she was going to take me to a lake. When she produced a rope and said we would play "higher and higher" I asked where the lake was. She said there wasn't one, and was I going to play "highrun highrun", as she pronounced it. I asked to be shown how. Then she got another little girl to hold one end of the rope while I held the other, and she jumped over it and we raised it about an inch after each jump, until she was out by not being able to jump it, and we took our turns. I soon told her this wasn't "highrun highrun", it was jumping, but she said they called it "highrun highrun", and thus I learned. When she called after me one day, "Whea's ta bahn?" I asked her what she meant, and she explained she meant where was I going. I often wished I was back at Kirk Hammerton where we all played the same games and everyone spoke alike.

It was my duty to come straight home from school and take Harry the baby for a little walk. I had to carry him, as we had no pram, so I usually took him as far as Cross Lane School, sat on the steps for a rest, and then brought him home. Then I would sit on the doorstep nursing him. After a while we would go in for tea: bread and marge with jam sometimes, and sometimes a piece of pie. We all came home for dinner, and how my mother managed to feed us all I just don't know, but there was always a tasty meal. In winter it would be sheep's head broth: half a sheep's head, boiled with turnip, onion, carrots and split peas, then simmered gently all the morning, and the result was wonderful. The broth was poured over a slice of bread that had been cut and diced into a basin. It satisfied our hunger. The vegetables were mashed and we had some of these later. If she couldn't get a sheep's head we had bone broth with dumplings, or a meat and potato pie, though the meat was a bit scarce. All the cooking was done on the kitchen range, gas ovens at this time being only for the affluent. Spotted Dick was one of our favourite puddings—a steamed suet pudding with currants in—and jam roly poly. My father's wage would be less than 30 shillings a week, I think about 23 shillings. The rent was about 5 shillings, coal 2 shillings, and there was the gas bill to save for. My two eldest sisters, who were in service at this time, would send any of their clothes home to be remade for us, and my mother would sit up well into the night altering and remaking so that we were sent out decent.

We joined the Methodist Sunday School, and I remember going on the Sunday School treat. We met at the School, lined up in fours, and marched round the district stopping in some of the streets to sing. We finally went into a field and all the children started chanting, "At our journey's end, we shall have a bun, we shall have a bun, we shall have a bun". However, we had to wait a while for our buns. First there were races for all ages: straight races, two-legged races, wheelbarrow races, skipping races, egg-and-spoon races. It was great fun and at last the tea urns came. We were told to line up, and we were all given a mug of tea and a long bun. And the long bun was what its name implied; it must have been at least 10 inches long, like a hot cross bun with currants in. I should find it very dry eating now but it was food of the Gods that day. After tea there was more racing, mostly by adults, who caused a lot of fun. Then the young people got down to the serious business of cricket, and we sat and watched till it was time to go home. We went home in groups with our Sunday School teachers, and all agreed we had a wonderful day.

We also looked forward to the children's service, in the chapel, at Whitsuntide. All the girls wore white dresses, and the boys white blouses, and we were packed tightly together on a platform and told not to wriggle. We all took part; there were special hymns which we alone sang, and some of us gave readings. The chapel was usually full, as our parents came to see us.

We used to do a lot of play acting, and someone or other would always be having a concert in someone's backyard. The price of admission was usually a pin, and if you hadn't one you were usually given one, which you duly paid in and you were admitted. These concerts were usually take-offs from some pantomime. (I had not seen a pantomime at this time.) The girls, who usually fancied themselves as Principal Boys, would stuff their dresses into their navy blue knickers, and then felt free to dance and sing. Sometimes they managed to get a chorus of three of four who would come on very lively in the opening chorus. I loved these concerts and always carried a pin round with me on the chance that I heard of one. All the old nursery rhymes were mimed, and the audience was left to guess who and what they were.

Another craze at this time was a pricking-in book. For this you cut out all the pretty pictures you could find, mostly advertisements, and then you put them between the pages of a book, which you carried round with you. You invited your friends to stick a pin between the pages; if they were lucky and inserted it where there was a picture, the picture became theirs and the pin became yours. The picture would usually go into their book, as we all carried them.

When we left Horton I was sorry to leave the blind boy who lived near us. We used to sit on the step and talk, and he used to feel for my plaits, because he said I talked like my brother Charles and he wanted to be sure he knew who he was talking to. His mother had always been very kind to me, and sometimes gave me a penny when I ran errands for her. The first time I went to the fish and chip shop for her I was told to ask for one of each four times and get back before the mill buzzer went. The counter was high and I was small and shy. There was no queuing as there is today; you just shouted up when it was your turn. I got pushed this way and that till an elderly woman said, "I think it's about time this little lass was served, she was here before me". "What d'ye want love?" I told the girl behind the counter, handed my money up, and received a huge parcel. I didn't know what was in it but I knew it smelt warm and good. It became a regular thing for me to go to the fish shop every Friday. Then one day the appetising smell was too much for me, and as I went home I poked open one corner of the parcel and found a chip, which I quickly popped in my mouth and burnt my throat with; but now I knew what chips were. Each week I would eat two or three, then quickly wipe my mouth before handing the parcel over. One day one of the girls, who had already got home from the mill and was waiting for her dinner, looked at hers, then at me, and said, "You've been eating them haven't you?" I blushed and stammered. She turned to her mother and said, "I told you last week there was hardly any chips on mine, but you wouldn't believe me". Her mother said, "Oh, get on with your dinner or you'll be late; I expect t'bairn was hungry". I ran home feeling like the thief I was. I didn't expect to have to go to the fish shop any more after that, but the following Friday the lady came round and asked me to go, and then she gave me another penny and said, "Now ask for a pennyworth of chips separate; then you can eat them on your way home and leave our Elsie's alone". Oh joy! I ran all the way there, and didn't those chips taste lovely! No need now to wipe my mouth and wonder if they could tell; these were mine, I could eat them all, then go home and have my dinner.

Chapter 4

South Parade

My parents were always on the lookout for a bigger house, and eventually we got one on South Parade, near Valley Parade football ground. The house was large. It had a basement kitchen with a keeping kitchen off the side. This kitchen or living room was large. It was about six steps down. It had a large window and was warm and dry. The floor was stone slabs. There was a stone sink, and a firegrate that absorbed many tins of black lead in its time, but always looked warm and cheery. The front room could be entered either by going up 13 steps from the cellar kitchen inside the house, or by going up 7 steps outside and entering by the front door, which opened onto a passage, the door for the room being on the left. The passage was wide and we found it very useful later on for storing our bicycles. At the end of this passage was a square landing with stairs leading up to the second floor. Two flights of steps, 14 in all, and another landing, with two bedrooms—but big ones; each would have taken two double beds. Another two flights of steps, 13 in all, another landing, and two attics. They were large and airy with only a little slope to the ceiling on the window side. Thus there were 40 steps from the cellar kitchen, where we lived, to the attics. This was a sobering thought, and taught us to remember when getting changed and so on to bring all we needed down with us. We moved in a few weeks before Christmas 1910 and we stayed there until 1933.

These houses were back-to-backs. As ours was a back house we went down a wide passage to it and had a piece of land, which we called a garden, and a yard. We tried to cultivate the garden now and again, never with much success. We looked onto the side of the Barracks. We had our own W.C., and altogether we thought we were very lucky to have got this house. The rent was six shillings a week. Later when the house came on the market we bought it.

My mother was much happier and set about making the house nice. It was quite a while before there was any money to spare for decorations, but every room was scrubbed from top to bottom. The kitchen was tackled

37

first, and we did manage to paper it. The floor was scrubbed and rubbed with scouring stone every Monday, after washday. During the winter we set about making tabbed rugs. The best parts of old coats were cut out and washed. They were then cut into strips about three-eighths of an inch wide, which were cut into pieces about three inches long. If it happened that we had a nice bright red or green, these colours were kept separate to make a pattern. We decided to make a special rug for the new house. It was two and a quarter yards long and a yard wide. My mother would never start till she had a sack full of clippings. With a coat from one person and an old dress from another at last the sack was full. The hessian that we pricked the mat on was now fixed to the frame, in such a way that it could be wound round when a piece was done. The frame rested between a box in the sink and the table, so that four of us could work on it at one time. We enjoyed doing this. A good fire would be built up to make the kitchen nice and warm, and we would aim to do a piece each night. While we were pricking we would sing or talk, and so the evening would pass. The clips were put into the hessian by making a hole with the prodder, a piece of wood about five inches long and half an inch thick, rounded and sharpened to a point at one end. The hole was made, the clip pulled through to half its length, another hole made, and the other half was pushed through this.

Each clip was put into the hold of the last clip, so the next fastened the last in and prevented them shaking out. Well, our particular rug grew during those winter nights and at last it was taken off the frame and laid on the floor, when we all jumped on it to claim that we were the first to be on it. It was grand: a black border about five inches wide, then a red triangle in each corner, and a red and green centre piece of double stars. These rugs were very hard wearing, and lovely and warm; we could all put our chairs up to the rug and get our feet on it on a winter's night.

It was now 1911. My father was working; Nellie was in the mill; George, who had been in farm service, now came home and got work in the mill; Bella was in service in Kent; Bessie and Annie were in service but got places in Bradford. My mother had applied for free dinners for us who were at school, Charlie, Alice and me. We were granted a three months' course, so soon after we started at Green Lane School we went along to the dinner centre each day. The dinners were good and we enjoyed them, but after the three months we were not granted any more. My father's wage of about 25s. a week, my sister's of 7s. 6d., and George's of about 10s. were supposed to be adequate for eleven of us. My mother always said that was the first and last time she ever asked for charity.

South Parade faced the City football ground, so we had the excitement of watching the people come to the football matches, also of being allowed in free at three-quarter time, not so much to watch the match as to scrounge round looking for empty cigarette packets and taking the cards out. We all collected cigarette cards, which were really entertaining and often very instructive. We were always short of money, but we had another source of income during the football season. We watched out for anyone coming to the match on a bicycle. We would then run up to them and say, "Mind your bike mister?" If he nodded yes we would run at his side and direct him into our yard. We charged 2*d.* each bike, and once at a cup-tie I had fifteen bikes and we should have had 2*s.* 6*d.*, but two slipped off without paying.

My older sisters helped my mother to make ends meet by sending their old clothes home, which my mother continued to cut down for us. Thus we were kept warm if not fashionable. Lizzie, who worked at John Holmes', was able through the housekeeper there to supply us with 7lb. jars of dripping, 1*s.* a jar. We children loved dripping and bread, so this was a boon. It became my job to go down for it. Sometimes I would go down before school and bring two jars. I used to carry one in each arm, so once I set off I couldn't change arms or scratch my ear or anything, until I got to Trafalgar Street. Here there was a house (where the Masonic Hall now stands) with a wall round just the right height. I could lower my jars onto the wall and have five minutes rest. I took all the dripping I could get, as we could always let some of the neighbours have a jar, and they usually gave me a penny or two for fetching it. The big fashionable houses at that time had their assistants living in, so that is how they came to have the dripping for sale. I suppose it was really "housekeeper's perks".

We gradually began to feel a bit better off, and one by one the rooms in the house were papered and painted, and oilcloth was laid on the floors, except in the kitchen, which was scrubbed and scoured for a long time yet. My sisters though working were not able to contribute anything to the family fund. They received about 15*s.* a month and of course their keep. Out of this they were required to provide uniforms: two print dresses and three plain white aprons for morning wear; one black dress, caps and cuffs, and three muslin aprons for afternoon. I suppose the first rig-out would cost about £4, or nearly three months' wages, so clothes were taken care of and patched carefully. They were given one night a week off, alternate Saturday afternoons and evenings, and Sunday afternoon and evenings. On Lizzie's day off she would usually come home, and there were three girls she brought home with her for a long time. They lived at Pocklington and were unable to go home very often. We

The author with her brothers and sisters c 1910
Back row: Nellie, George, Annie
Seated: Bessie
Front row: Charlie, Jim, Alice, Maggie
(Photo courtesy James Ogden)

were all encouraged to bring our friends home, and there would often be fourteen to tea on Sunday nights.

I liked Green Lane School. At first the size of it overwhelmed me. It had what seemed to be a huge hall. The headmaster, Mr. Jonathan Priestley, J.B. Priestley's father, was very quick-tempered and often caned first and asked afterwards. The old man never spoke well of his son, who however used to come in and take classes sometimes. These classes were popular, because J.B. had enlightened ideas, according to my sister Ethel. He once set them an essay, describe any well known school character. They nearly all chose to write about Mr. Priestley, his bald head encircled by white hair, his red face and bad temper. J.B. laughed at the essays, and encouraged the class to laugh too, which at the time was most unusual for a schoolteacher. Mr. Priestley gave us a talk about saving, and said he was starting a savings bank in conjunction with the Yorkshire Penny Bank; we had to ask our mothers if we could join. We could put in as little as a penny, and few of us ever took more than threepence. I was very proud of that Bank Book and was always reckoning it up; when it reached £1 it was transferred to the Yorkshire Penny Bank, and I did want to reach £1 before I left school. In 1912 my brother Charles started working half-time, and then the neighbours would look at me and say it would be my turn next. I was looking forward to working. I always wanted to earn some money; it seemed to me you couldn't do much without it. I always remembered my mother crying at having to leave Kirk Hammerton, and she wouldn't have had to do so if she had had money.

We went to Carlisle Road Methodist Sunday School, and our life revolved round this a good deal. They ran a Band of Hope Meeting on Saturday nights, which was very popular. We were shown lantern slides, told stories on the evils of drink, and always had some good rousing hymns with choruses. We owe a lot to the dedicated workers who gave us those happy Saturday nights. We paid a penny, and were given prizes at the end of the year for good attendance. Christmas we always had a party, and the nearest Saturday to Plot Night we were regaled with parkin, toffee and milk. We went to Sunday School morning and afternoon, but to me it was never quite as friendly as Kirk Hammerton. Perhaps I was shy, and it was of course much bigger. Our Sunday School outing was the great event of the year, when seats were fixed to coal wagons and we were taken to a field at Esholt for games and tea. We once had a class trip to Knaresborough. It was a beautiful day and it was the first time I had been to Knaresborough. I knew it was only nine miles from Kirk Hammerton, and I had a great longing to leave the party

Three sisters—Hetty, Alice and Lillian—on the steps at South Parade *c* 1920
(Photo courtesy of Margaret Walter)

and go see the old place. I really felt homesick. I remember my class
teachers; they really took an interest in us. I remember Miss Barrett and
Miss Dobson with love and respect.

When I was about fifteen I stopped going to Carlisle Road, I don't just
know why, and instead went with my sister to Eastbrook Hall in the
evenings, and then on to the open-air meetings on the Wool Exchange
steps in Market Street. Market Street was a Sunday night "prom", where
young folks walked up and down to get to know each other. It seems
unbelievable now, but at that time there was no means of meeting people
of the opposite sex except at chapel or work. There were no youth clubs, so
young people made these "proms"; at Bradford, on Market Street, Toller
Lane and Manningham Lane. Sometimes the crowds were so great that

the police had hard work to keep them moving. Gilbert Muir, the Minister at Eastbrook Hall, started holding open-air meetings to try to get the young folk to go to the Mission, and no doubt quite a lot did, but they still had nowhere to go afterwards. We were fortunate in that we had a front room and were encouraged to take our friends home, to talk, read or play games.

I was still at school when I got my first regular job. The housekeeper at John Holmes' asked me if I would go to her sister's and wash the front steps for her on Friday evenings. They lived quite near us, so off I went. Mrs. Hutchinson was a semi-invalid, and always wore a dressing gown. I washed the steps, and sometimes the oilcloth round the living room, and did errands. She gave me 9*d.* a week, and a pot of cocoa with two slices of bread and *butter.* She used to like me to sit and talk as she never had any company; her husband was a waiter at a hotel and never got home till nearly midnight.

Our neighbour who lived up the same passage as us was an elderly lady, Mrs. Simpson, who always lived in one room. Sometimes I would go in when she asked me to go to the shop for her, and I never saw a room with so much furniture or so many pictures on the wall. There must have been at least fifty, and some of them were really good; she had bought them when she was better off. Every Monday morning this old lady went with a large bundle to Uncle's, a pawn shop on Westgate. On Friday she would go and redeem the things she had pawned. She was always hard up and used to try to sell her trinkets. She gave me a pretty teapot once for going errands, which I still have.

In the house in front of us lived an elderly couple with a grown-up daughter. Next to them lived a couple where the husband worked in a shop and was the perfect shop-assistant, very deferential. On the way home he invariably got drunk, and if his supper was not to his fancy he would take the four corners of the tablecloth, lift up the lot and put it on the fire. All the family were afraid of him except his eldest daughter. She would have left home, but felt she had a duty to her mother and her sister, who was a cripple and also suffered from tuberculosis, as indeed all the family did.

We played all the usual games on the street. There was very little traffic in those days, and every street was a playground. The boys used to play "Piggy", a game something like Knurr and Spell. A "piggy", a stick about seven inches long and about as thick as a fire chip, was balanced on a stone. The boy then hit one end, and as the stick flew in the air he gave it a whack; then he would see how many hop-skip-and-jumps it took him to reach it. One of our favourite games was "Tin Can Squat" or "Relievo". The one who was "it" was usually decided by some "dip" such as

> My little pussy cat likes new milk.
> Does your little pussy cat like new milk?

You answered "yes" or "no", and the "dip" continued:

> NO spells no, so you are not it.

And so we went on with the rhyme, touching every player as the words were said, until by a process of elimination we found out who was "it". Sometimes the rhyme would be:

> Eena meena mina mo
> Catch a nigger by the toe
> If he screams let him go
> Eena meena mina mo

Then the game started. A tin was placed on a stone in the middle of the street. Then "it", standing with eyes closed and hands over eyes, started to count 20, and we all ran and hid. When "it" had finished counting he shouted "coming", and if he spotted one of us he called the name, and both ran back to the "homey". If you managed to get there first you kicked the can away and called "relievo", when everyone came out and "it" was "it" again. You could also run out and relieve everyone if you saw that "it" was a long way from the can. If however "it" got there first then you were "it".

Chapter 5

In The Mill

But time was moving on and I was nearly twelve. My mother asked Nellie to "ask on" for me at the mill, which she did. I was assured of a job as soon as I reached my twelfth birthday. I was quite excited and eager to start work. At last the day arrived. I awoke; was it time to get up? My sister, who slept beside me, didn't stir. A few minutes passed. Then my mother called, "Annie, Nellie, it's time to get up". It was ten minutes to six. Annie stirred beside me and said, "Come on, our Maggie, you don't want to be late first morning". Nellie, who slept in the other single bed in the room, was already dressing. I started to dress quickly. My thoughts were far ahead of me. This was it! Today I started work; soon I would be bringing a wage home, and all my mother's money troubles would be over. I was twelve and grown up. I hurried downstairs. My mother had made the fire, and had packed sandwiches for our breakfasts. I had a quick wash at the kitchen sink, then poured a cup of tea and sat down to eat a slice of bread and jam. Then we were off. I went with Nellie, who was a spinner and had asked for me to start as a half-timer. I was excited; I had heard such tales about the mill, and now I was really going. We joined some more girls on the way, who looked at me and then turned to Nellie and asked, "She your sister?" Nellie answered, "Yes". They said "She's a little un". They asked me if I wanted to work in the mill. I answered "yes", because it was expected of me. "You'll soon be wishing you were out." "Oh, I don't know", piped up another girl, "sometimes we have fun, and anyway there's always the wage on Friday. I get four and six and my mother gives me threepence a week spending money." This sounded great; up to now I had never had more than a penny a week.

We turned in at the mill gates and were soon climbing up the steps to "No. 3". The warm air met you as you entered. Nellie said, "Come on, you'd better put your coat in my locker, but you'll be doffing". I walked down the room very close to her. There was an aisle down the centre; the spinning frames were on either side. There were great big wheels and belts overhead, with pulleys connected to the machines. All of a sudden the

45

wheels started turning, slowly at first, then gaining momentum faster and faster. The women came out and started work. The noise was terrifying. I wanted to cry, I wanted to hide, but most of all I wanted to run, to run right away. Nellie turned and saw my frightened face. "Come on, there's nothing to be frightened of, you'll soon get used to the noise." I couldn't tell her this all seemed evil to me; I just couldn't speak.

George the overlooker passed and stood at the top of the "gate" (the opening between two machines). He looked at Nellie. "So this is your sister! She's a little un. Well, she'd better get started." Then, turning to me: "Well, this is better than school, isn't it, *and* you get paid for it". I said "yes", again because it was expected of me. "Well, you'd better go and see old Harriet. She'll soon put you in the way. Come on!" I followed him to a machine that was stopped. On each side were three young doffers, girls about my own age, and one older woman. She seemed very old to me. Her face and nose, which was very large, were always blue. She swore a lot and was dirty and untidy. "Here Harriet, I've brought you another one. See what you can do with her." And George walked away. Harriet said, "Don't be frightened love, you'll soon learn it. Now we've finished here, so I'm going to set the machine on. Mind your plaits don't get round the rollers; it would fetch your scalp off as clean as a whistle. I should put your plaits under your pinny." We all wore black "pinnies" or aprons, which fastened down the back; I loosened mine, put my plaits in, and fastened it up again.

Now Harriet had started the machine. The doffers just stood by their own share, picked up any broken ends, and joined them again. When all the ends were spinning, Harriet called "come on", and we all went to another machine that was awaiting our service. A spinning machine takes the wool that has already been processed to the thickness of thick wool, known as "rovings", and spins it to the thickness of thick cotton. When the bobbins receiving the spun rovings are full, the doffers are called to take the bobbins off and put empty ones in their place. Harriet showed me how to do this. "Break the thread off, then fix it, under the empty bobbin a turn, just to fix the bobbin, and that's all there is to it. Always see that your bobbin is fixed tight. You're alright. Put your full bobbin on the peg where you took the empty one off; John will be coming to take them away. Then young Charlie comes and puts empty ones on the rail again, ready for the next doffing." We had finished again now, and Harriet was just setting the machine on. When John came for the bobbins he bumped into Harriet and said, "Hello, old blue nose". She turned round but he quickly got out of reach. She called after him, "You cheeky young bugger!" But John only laughed and kept touching his nose.

Harriet turned to me. "He's a cheeky bugger; you don't want to have aught to do with him. You're Nellie's sister aren't you? Now she's a nice lass. There's no more want doffing just now; come on, we'll sit down a minute." We all went down to the end of the room and sat down. I knew one of the girls; she went to my school. "Well, how are you liking it?" she asked. "Oh alright." "Oh," she said, "it's alright at first,"—she had been working about six months— "but you get fed up with it. I'm going to get out when I'm fourteen, and learn dress-making or millinery. My mother says I can." Just then someone shouted, "doff here!" and we all trooped down to the machine.

We had just finishing doffing the machine, when John walked down the aisle with a tray, shouting "tea!" Everyone fetched their pint pots, containing their mashings of tea and sugar. John took them to fill them with hot water. When he got back the great wheels were slowing down and stopping. The spinners turned their machines off and everyone went to their buffets by the window, took their sandwiches out, and started eating their breakfasts. Breakfast was from 8 to 8.30. "Well", said Nellie, "How are you getting on?" "Oh, alright. Harriet says I'll soon be on my own share. She smells and swears." "I know", said Nellie, "but don't you say anything about it. Can you reach the bobbin rail?" "Only by standing on tiptoe, and it does make your legs ache." "Well, you'll grow. Now I'm going to read for ten minutes. There's a *Magnet* or *Gem* in the locker if you want to read it." I took the *Magnet* and had got interested in Harry Wharton and the Famous Five when the wheels started and the books were put away. Nellie set her machine on and I went to join Harriet. We carried on with the doffing until 12.30 when the engine stopped for forty minutes for dinner. We then ran for our coats and ran most of the way home. Dinner was ready. My sisters returned to work. I helped to wash up, then went upstairs and changed for school. My mother said, "Well, how did you like it?" I said, "alright", and tried to convince myself that I really did like it.

I began to feel very tired and hoped we shouldn't have drill. The first lesson was arithmetic, which I managed to cope with. The second was geography, and my mind kept wandering back to the mill. After playtime we were told to take out our books and read. This was fine at first; then I started nodding and soon my head fell on the desk and I was asleep. After a while the teacher came round and tapped me gently on the fingers. I awoke, rubbed my eyes, and picked up the book. "Well, if you've had your afternoon siesta Maggie, we will now get on with the lesson." The class laughed, not unkindly. "Now will you start reading at the third chapter, and might I suggest that you go straight to bed tonight?" Soon the lesson was over. The bell went and we all marched into the main hall, where we sang "Now the day is over". A short prayer, and we were dismissed.

We ran home and immediately started getting tea ready. Usually it was bread and dripping, or bread and margarine and jam, but today was Monday and we always had warm oven cakes and bacon, with lots of dip; we dipped our cakes in and it was great. We finished off with a piece of jam cake and a cup of tea, and were then ready for any mischief. The table was now prepared again for my father and the older members of the family who would soon be home from work. In the meantime we went out to play. We soon collected some friends and started a game of Tin Can Squat. This continued till a few of the neighbours came out and told us to stop kicking that can about. Three of us went for a walk as far as the park. We sat on a seat and I told the other two what a wonderful place the mill was, and how rich I was going to be, and generally enlarged on all the day's happenings. We returned home about 7.30. My younger sisters met me and told me I'd got to go in, as I'd got to go to bed at 8.00 in order to get up in time for work in the morning. I went in. My mother said, "Well you'd better get washed, and if you want any supper get it; then off you go to bed, you're a worker now. Don't pick that book up, you've no time for that now." I washed and got myself a slice of jam and bread and a cup of water. I was allowed to look at my book while I ate my supper. I made it last as long as I could, then said goodnight and went off to bed.

In the darkness I went over the events of the day. Did I like the mill? I wasn't sure. It meant more money, and we had always been short. When I said my prayers I had almost added, "and please take me out of the mill", but this would have seemed ungrateful. Did people really go on in the mill, day after day, year after year? I had heard of people who had worked in the same mill, doing the same job, over thirty years. I knew I didn't want that. Perhaps when I was fourteen something else would turn up. It was no use worrying. I turned over and went to sleep.

The following week I was on afternoon turn at the mill. I hurried home from school, got my dinner, changed, made my bed, came down and found I had a few minutes to spare; so I picked up a *Magnet* and got on with the adventures of Greyfriars School until Nellie had finished her dinner. The afternoon seemed very long; we started at 1.10 and carried on without a break till 5.40. We joked amongst ourselves and sang all the popular songs. George the overlooker would walk down the aisles three or four times waving his alley-strap and cracking it on the floor; this sent all the fluff flying under the spinning frames and gave

The Children's Reading Room, Mannigham Library, 1911.
(Photo courtesy Bradford Libraries)

the room a swept up appearance. The alley-strap was a piece of leather about 27 inches long and 10 inches broad; it was fixed to a handle, and when swung round and hitting the floor with a violent whack it became a most fearsome thing. I was always afraid of it. I suppose that is why it cracked so often near me when I was least expecting it. I have seen George whang it round the boys when they misbehaved; he also used to get hold of them by the ear and make them wriggle. There wasn't a lot of violence; if there were any arguments it was best to keep your voice down, or the alley-strap would settle them. There was quite a bit of swearing went on, but George soon pulled the boys up if they swore at us girls, though some of the girls could swear as hard as the boys. We were not a swearing family; I never heard my parents use bad language, and the Sunday School had instilled it into me that the wages of sin was the everlasting fire, so I had no wish to swear. At 5.40 we were all ready with our coats on, and as soon as the engine stopped we made one mad rush for the stairs and freedom.

We would hurry home, have tea, then go out and play till bedtime. Sometimes we would have a walk to the library, where we could take a book out and sit in a comfortable chair in a warm room to read it. I think

I went through all Mrs. O. J. Walton's books at Manningham Library. They were all very sad, and tears used to roll down my face while I read. It was awful when closing time came and you were in the middle of a story; you had to hand it in and come again the following night to read how your hero had gone on. Sometimes in the evening the barrel organ man would come round. Then we would all gather round and listen while he played his entire repertoire, consisting of about six pieces; sometimes we would dance or sing to them. Then once or twice the German Band came with a couple of dancing bears. At the end of these performances we would go and beg pennies from our mothers for the performers. A rag-and-bone man used to come round and pay us threepence or fourpence a dozen for jam jars.

I was quite well-off now, and would sometimes treat myself to a quarter of sweets to eat in the mill; it was surprising how they helped the time along. I was also able to buy my own hair ribbons and sometimes a pair of stockings. I longed for the day when I could have a pair of shoes instead of boots. My father used to say they were "fool things, and no one in their right senses would buy them". Nevertheless I still wanted shoes, so I would save for them myself, but 6s.11d. takes a lot of saving in pennies and threepences. It was the thing in those days to get your new clothes for Whitsuntide, and I got my new shoes when I got my new clothes; my mother found the difference between what I had saved and what I needed. Our new clothes were only worn on Sundays; they had to last and look smart till next Whitsuntide, when they would be taken for second-best.

On Saturday nights in summer we would sometimes have a walk round the markets. We got great fun listening to the salesmen. There was a medicine man whose voice you could hardly hear, till he took a dose of his own medicine, when it miraculously returned with all the volume of a Sergeant-Major. "Now take a bottle home with you and you'll be fit as a fiddle after a couple of doses", he would yell. On Saturday nights in winter we continued to go to the Band of Hope. We really enjoyed these meetings, chiefly for the singing.

We were always saving up for holidays, and our savings usually amounted to a shilling or two. At Easter we would have a day on Shipley Glen, often spending up and having four weary miles to walk home. On Whit Monday we usually got up to watch the walkers. They set off on a 40 mile walk at 9 a.m. We would be up on Manningham Lane at 8.30 to get a good position. It's surprising now to think of how excited we got waiting for the first man to appear. First there were the programme sellers, then the collectors, as this was done to help the hospital. Then came cars with first-aid equipment, cars advertising Bovril, and the police on horseback keeping the crowds back. Everyone wanted to be the first to see the first walker. Eventually he was spotted and a cheer went up. The walkers were not spread out much here, so now there would be a bunch of them, and perhaps a few stragglers, some already blowing from their walk up Darley Street. We used to pass remarks about their skinny legs and on the way they used their arms. We were quite sure we could do as well as they, but I don't remember any of us trying.

In the afternoon some of us would be going on the Sunday School outing. We would meet outside the Sunday School, where there would be coal carts swept and washed, with seats from the school fastened on. We piled onto these and were taken sometimes to Apperley Bridge and sometimes to Baildon. How far away those places seemed at that time! When we went to Baildon we all had to get off at the bottom of Browgate, as the horses couldn't pull us up the hill. The excitement was intense all the way. We were certain someone would fall off, or the wagon would break, or a wheel would come off, or the horse would drop dead; but I don't remember any of these things ever happening. When we reached the moors we were told to keep together; very soon games and races were arranged and we were all kept busy. Tea consisted of a mug of tea, a long bun, and usually an iced bun. After tea there were races for the grown-ups, with us sitting round making rude remarks, and probably a cricket match. At about 6.30 we set off home, and we were back in time to get to some vantage point to watch the fireworks going up in Peel Park. Yes, Whit Monday was a very full day, and there must have been a lot of happy but tired people at the end of it.

I now started going to the Oak Lane Cinema on Saturday afternoons. This was known as "the penny rush". We were a noisy, excited crowd of children, out to enjoy ourselves. When the pictures started there was quiet, except for the oohs and ahs as our heroes and heroines got in and out of fearful predicaments, but the noise was really great when the comics came on: Charlie Chaplin, Buster Keaton and Harold Lloyd. It was usual to have a serial, so each week the hero or heroine was left in some predicament, perhaps bound and gagged in a cellar with water already a foot high and still pouring in, or hanging over the edge of a cliff with some horrible jagged rocks to fall on. So when the serial came on there was a great cheer, and we all sat and gasped as the rescue came just in time.

The next holiday was the annual week when the mill closed down. This was what we had been saving for, and there was a great holiday pay-out at the mills the week before we broke up. Some people managed to have a week at the seaside; Blackpool, Morecambe and Bridlington were the most popular places. Bed and breakfast was about four shillings a night, and most of the workers catered for themselves, taking the food in for the landlady to cook it. I remember talking to one young woman in the mill, who was reckoning her money up and wondering how far it would go. When she said, "And there's two shillings for t'clock", I asked her what she meant. She said, "Why everybody leaves two shillings under t'clock for when they come home. They know they'll come back penniless, but if there's two bob under t'clock you can always send out for fish and chips, and well, tomorrow's another day." There were no 'holidays with pay', so apart from the cost of the holiday there was the week without pay to be considered.

I went to relatives at South Milford for my holidays, and thought it was grand. My Uncle Joe, my mother's brother, was a great tease. He had a moustache like Lord Kitchener's. South Milford is a small village about 14 miles from Leeds. There was nothing much to do, but my auntie took me round, and we went for walks. I used to like to go and see the frogs in the stream.

After the holidays it wasn't long before we started thinking about Christmas presents. Most of us joined a Christmas Club and paid a penny or twopence a week, to get a box of chocolates for Christmas. We would buy a few packets of crimped paper, which we cut and made into streamers to decorate the room at the mill. We would have a walk round at dinner time to see the other rooms and decide which we liked best. As Christmas drew near there was always someone singing carols during meal-times. Someone would start "Hark the herald angels sing" or "While shepherds watched", and soon it was taken up by another and another, till soon almost everyone had joined in. It was in the mill that I was introduced to Handel's *Messiah*. Most of the mill workers, if they could sing, would be taking part in the *Messiah* at their own places of worship. They put in a bit of practice while working. It was quite common to hear snatches of "Unto us a Child is born", "He was despised", and the Alleluia Chorus, sung and whistled. I knew one girl who could almost go through the whole score. I wished I could sing. I should be thirteen the first time I went to hear the *Messiah*, but I have been many times since.

Singing carols was another way of making a few pence, and after tea two or three of us would go round carol singing; it was quite possible to hear three or four lots of carollers singing at once. We always started with:

> Here we come a-wassailing, among the leaves so green,
> And here we come a-wandering, so fair to be seen;
> For it is our Christmas time, when we travel far and near,

> To wish you all good health, and a happy new year,
> A new year, a new year,
> We wish you all good health, and a happy new year!

If we managed to be allowed to get so far, we continued with two or three carols, finishing off with:

> We are not daily beggars, that beg from door to door,
> But we are neighbours' children that you have seen before;
> For it is our Christmas time, when we travel far and near,
> To wish you all good health, and a happy new year,
> A new year, a new year,
> We wish you all good health, and a happy new year!

We would then knock, and if there was no response we would give them another verse:

> God bless the master of this house, and bless the mistress too,
> And all the little children, who round the table go;
> For it is our Christmas time, when we travel far and near,
> To wish you all good health, and a happy new year,

and then again the chorus. If there was still no response we would give them our final piece:

> A hole in my stocking, a hole in my shoe,
> Please can you spare a copper or two?
> If you haven't a penny a ha'penny will do,
> If you haven't a ha'penny, God bless you!

We would give one loud final knock, and if this didn't produce anything we would walk off and try somewhere else.

Chapter 6

A Day in 1915

It was in 1913 that rumours of war began to float around. We didn't pay too much attention; we were too young. We did pay attention to the Suffragette Movement; we found something funny in the idea of votes for women. They had a meeting room in what used to be a shop on Manningham Lane. Whenever we were passing, if there were signs of activity there, we would walk very quietly up to the door, open it quickly and all yell together, "votes for women" in a derisory way. It was one way of letting off steam. But as time went on the war clouds grew thicker and we began to talk of the Germans as our enemies. Then one day it happened; we were at war. On 4th August 1914 I was thirteen and still working half-time; the following April I should be going full time. We lived near the barracks, which during the last few months had been repaired, and now boys of eighteen were coming there to be fitted out for the Royal Artillery. On Sunday mornings there was a church parade led by a band playing their signature tune, "The British Grenadiers". A brass band will always draw children, and we lined up to watch. We were soon to see some of the uglier aspects of war, when gangs of hooligans went and broke windows of shops owned by Germans. These shopkeepers were in the main good honest people, who had served us well with their pork shops and delicatessens. Some had omitted to get naturalised, and were taken away to internment camps. We had quite a lot of Germans in Bradford who had worked hard for the good of the city, but all came under suspicion and were looked upon as possible spies.

Now things speeded up in the mills, and instead of spinning the good botany wool for which Bradford was famous we were spinning a rough yarn which had already been dyed either khaki or blue—all part of the speeding-up process. This gave off much more fluff, and we were usually covered at the end of the day in fine hairs. The machines were also speeded up. Some of the overlookers had already joined the army, and soon the shortage of manpower began to make itself felt.

In April 1915 I reached the age of fourteen and left school. I knew now that I did not want to work in the mill, but what else could I do?

On leaving school we were encouraged to go to night school, so I decided I would join evening classes at the beginning of the next session, in September, and see if I could learn something that would help me to do some other work; meanwhile I carried on in the spinning. The days seemed very long, and I was often too tired to go out and play in the evenings, so if the night was fine I would sit on the doorstep with *The Gem* or *The Magnet*. I also used to like playing checks. There were four checks and a bouncer for this game. You sat on the floor and scattered the checks. Then, throwing up the bouncer, you repeated the rhyme:

> Sweep the floor,
> Sweep it clean,
> Pick up a chair,
> And place it there.

Suiting the action to the words, you twice swept the floor with your finger tips and picked up the bouncer after it had bounced; then you picked up a check. This was repeated till all four had been collected. They were then scattered again, and this time you endeavoured to pick up two checks before catching the bouncer. Then you tried for three, and four. You were out if you failed to pick the required number of checks or if you missed the bouncer. I spent hours sitting on the cold flagstones, determined to go through without cheating.

Sometimes I talked with other girls about the war and the young men who had already gone. The glory of it was beginning to fade. The first few boys had come home on leave, looking much older, and not wanting to talk about the trenches, but just to go to the pictures, onto the moors, or round the park, and to forget that in a few days they would have to go back.

One day in 1915 I remember well. It began much the same as the others. "Maggie, Maggie! It's nearly ten past six! You'll be late if you don't look sharp, and you know you were late once last week. For goodness sake get up! I'm going downstairs now and I'll pour your tea out so that it will be getting cool. Are you awake? I shan't wait for you, I shall go as soon as I'm ready. I'm off now, get up won't you?" This was Nellie. "Yes, yes, I'll get up now." I threw the clothes back, stretched, yawned, got out, and reached for my clothes. I knew by experience that I could dress in less than three minutes, and in less than five I had run down the 40 steps from attic to kitchen and was having a quick wash by the kitchen sink. The cold water stung my cheeks and gave me a clean fresh feeling, but as I

"I still worked at Drummond's"
(Photo courtesy Stroud Riley Drummond Co Ltd)

reached for the tea my sister had poured out I would have given all I possessed to have been able to go back to bed and have my sleep out. Just to stay there till I woke without an alarm clock or someone calling would have been heaven. I had a slice of jam and bread, finished my tea, put my coat on, and picked up a parcel of sandwiches my mother had packed.

My father had to be at work at 6 a.m., so my mother got up at 5 a.m., lit the fire, made tea, and packed sandwiches for him and the three working sisters. Then she called us and went back to bed till 7.30, when she got up again and got the three younger children off to school. Then her day really began.

Nellie and I worked at the same mill, and could make the journey in nine minutes. Nellie didn't like to have to hurry. Neither did I, but I could not resist holding onto my bed till the last minute. I glanced at the clock; it was turning twenty past six. I would run to the end of the street, walk up the hill, and then along the back street. I could shut my eyes while going along this back street, and get the feeling that I was having another little sleep. Then I would hurry along the last stretch and just make it. I arrived at the mill just as the pennyhoilman was closing the gate. He smiled and said, "You've nobbut just made it. I should get off early to bed tonight". I grinned and hurried on. I still had six flights of steps to climb to get to No. 3, and the thought of the overlooker and his alley-strap spurred me on. I arrived a bit breathless just as the engine went on and the wheels began to turn. I rolled my coat up and put it in the locker at the bottom of the gate. From the other end of the room I saw George come out of his gate. I turned my machine on slowly to avoid breaking any ends. George passed me, swishing the alley-strap. I was well down the gate and out of reach of it, busy watching my ends and mending any that broke. I was a spinner now and minded three sides, a frame and a half. When the bobbins of spun rovings were full I stopped the machine and shouted "Doff here!" From somewhere three or four doffers appeared. They took the full bobbins off, letting them drop into leather tubs which they pushed along with their feet, and replacing them with empty ones. Then the machine was set on again. The noise was terrible, and to see all the wheels going round was frightening at first, but familiarity breeds contempt and most spinners never heard the noise. We had no chance of talking, as we couldn't leave our sides, but occasionally we would call a greeting to somebody nearby. We often sang as we worked; I was sadly out of tune but as nobody could hear it didn't matter.

At breakfast we had our sandwiches and tea with sugar but no milk. Milk meant bringing a bottle from home, or using condensed, so most people did without. My breakfast usually consisted of a bacon sandwich and two jam ones, three slices in all. Sometimes I had a piece of jam or mince pasty. The tea boy was allowed to go out to the shop ten minutes before meal times, to fetch things in, such as pasties and teacakes at breakfast time, or fish and chips at dinner time. My friend joined me and we would talk of where we had been at the week-end, or of boys we knew, or of what was going on at our local chapel. This morning Hilda told me of rumours that the mill was going on overtime. It was an exciting topic. How long should we work and how much extra should we get? Some of the older women who were accustomed to lie down on the stone floor after breakfast and have a sleep till the engine went on again soon told us to talk quietly.

All too soon the wheels started turning and the engine was on again. George would walk down the alley shouting, "Ger 'em on!" — meaning start the spinning frames — and in two minutes all the spindles were spinning again. Sometimes the morning seemed endless and everyone was watching the clock; as it neared 12.30 coats were slipped on and people got ready to dash out as soon as the engine stopped. The boys and girls all ganged up as they left the mill, laughing and talking just because it was so good to be out. I went home for dinner and usually ran most of the way. Dinner was ready, the table was nicely set with a clean cloth, and the food was good and wholesome though we could afford only the cheaper cuts of meat. Soon the mill buzzers were hooting, telling everyone it was five to one; dinners were hurriedly finished and back we went. We met our friends on the way, linked arms, and walked on together, sometimes being annoyed by the boys who would pull our plaits. Most of us wore coats with just little head shawls for the cold weather. Older women wore long shawls which were really warm and could also be used on the bed at night. Most of us wore clogs which were warm and comfortable; but we young ones thought clogs and shawls old fashioned, and longed for shoes and coats.

Back in the mill everything was quiet. Some of the women were lying on the floor having a sleep. There was always a temptation for the boys to make a clatter, when half-a-dozen irate women would tell them in no uncertain language to stop the din; and if the overlooker happened to be awakened too they would most likely get their ears pinched and a taste of the alley-strap. At 1.10 the wheels started and the frames were set going again; then it was watching, picking up the ends, a little singing, and perhaps just thinking. I used to let my mind wander; it cost nothing to dream. Sometimes I would imagine myself a film star, and would plan what to do with my fabulous wage. First there would be a large house in the country, with someone to help mother with the work. There would be trips to the seaside; up to now I had not seen the sea. My younger sisters would go to the grammar school, and there would be lots of nice clothes. We should have a bathroom. But I wouldn't keep all the money; I would help all the poor people I knew. Then my mind would wander to the lovely walks round Bradford, where I had been at the week-end. How lovely Chellow Dene looked when the trees were in leaf and the bluebells were making a carpet! Or Manningham Park, with the flower beds and flowering shrubs, the promenade round the bandstand, the bands which played there on Saturdays and Sundays, the lakeside walk where you met your friends and sometimes made new ones.

Saturday night was the highlight of the week, though I enjoyed Sundays, with an extra two or three hours in bed, and lovely bacon and hot oven cakes for breakfast, eaten in a nice and leisurely way. Then Sunday School; the dressing up for it and the quiet reverent feeling I always got on entering. Saturday was different; we had fun. This week I was going with my friend to the Mechanics' Institute. We would have to be down early as it was bound to be full. There was a good concert

Chellow Dene, 1903
(Photo courtesy Bradford Libraries)

party coming with a marvellous tenor singer and a girl who was such a clever dancer; each week different pierrot troupes came, some better than others. It was 4d. in the balcony and you had a good view and a comfortable seat. The audience was quick to show appreciation of a good act and to boo at a poor one. This brought me up to my arithmetic: 4d. for the Mechanics', 2d. for sweets, and a penny for chips when we came home: 7d. My spending money was a penny in the shilling earned. My wage was 10s. 6d. so I had 10½d. a week and my mother made it up to the shilling. I still had 9d. a week from Mrs. Hutchinson: 1s. 9d. Out of the 1s. 2d. left, 2d. would go in the collection on Sunday, 6d. would be saved for my holiday; then there was the occasional birthday card (1d.) or bus ride to be accounted for. In the winter we went to the Eastbrook Hall Methodist Mission Sunday evening services, and swelled the funds there by another penny.

I was brought back to the present with a start when I heard old Mrs. Smith call "I'll be with you in a minute Maggie", and realised that my rovings on the other side were running out. I would have to be very quick and put new rovings on as soon as the old ones were finished.

There was a tub of new rovings at the top of the gate. Mrs. Smith, who was nearly 70, was the roving setter up, and came to help. As we worked we talked. Mrs. Smith said, "Nay Maggie, you were miles away. Is it some lad you're thinking about?" "No, it isn't", I answered, "I don't bother wi't'lads. I was thinking about Saturday night; we're going to the Mechanics'." "Eh you'd better be going for a walk and getting some good fresh air in your lungs." "Oh, we're going for a walk on Sunday after Sunday School to Chellow Dene. I like it there." "Yes, I know Chellow Dene. I used to go there, and I used to look at those great big mansions with their great conservatories, all owned by millowners related to each other. Just have a look when you go. That's where you live when you own a mill. Then come down and have a look at White Abbey and think that's where you live when you work in the mill and are glad to take ten shillings home on a Friday. But you'll see better days. Our unions are getting stronger, and we shall soon be getting a bit more, or there will be strikes." "What's a strike?" I asked. "Well, that's when you've asked for a rise in wages and the millowners won't listen. Then if we were all of one mind and could withdraw our labour, well, where would they be without any workers?" "But we should have no money", I said, "how would we live?" "Well, that's just it. Now if everyone joined the union and paid their twopence or threepence a week, then the unions would be strong and be able to pay out a few shillings a week while the workers were on strike, and the bosses wouldn't have it all their own way. We should have union men to speak for us. But you won't always stay in the mill; isn't there anything else you want to do?" "Yes, lots", I said, "but they would be less wage. Eight shillings a week in shops and about five for dressmaking. I'd be worse off." "Well", said Mrs. Smith, "I've worked in t'mill ower fifty years. I was only ten when I first went in a mill and I'm still here, but thank goodness my lads are out. One's a plumber and the other's a joiner, and there's only me left now, so I shall keep coming as long as I can. Your brother's left; how's he going on? Went onto the railway didn't he? Well, he'll be alright there; he was a steady lad." "Oh yes," I said, "Charlie's working on the railway and really likes it. Have you heard whether we are going on overtime?" "I don't know, but I shouldn't be surprised. Well, I think we've got them all going now, I'll be off, and just you remember; get off to night school and get yourself something different to the mill."

This set me thinking. I knew I wanted to get out of the mill, but how? I had always thought I might get out when I was fourteen, but now I was fourteen and still here. I intended going to evening classes in September. I could go free the first year after leaving school, and if my attendance was good I should win a prize and a free pass for the next year.

The afternoon wore on. The "walking boss", the man one step above the overlookers, came round and held a little conference with them. Then the overlookers came round to us, and told us that as from next Monday we should be working over; there was no exemption for anyone except the half-timers. We were all excited and managed to meet each other and have a quick word. We were to stop at 5.40 as usual, have a ten minutes' break, then work from 5.50 till 7.50, and for this we were to receive another 2s. 1d. I thought how lovely it would be taking home the extra money and getting more spending money. We were told it would be for about six weeks, and they didn't want any more people being pennied because of this.

Being pennied was having a penny taken off your wage for being late. At 6.30 the pennyhoilman would start closing the gate; if you managed to get through before it closed you were alright. Some pennyhoilmen would close it slowly if they saw you running. If it was closed you had to go through the pennyhoil, the office by the gate. Your name was taken by the pennyhoilman, and a penny would be docked from your wage. If you had three pennies off in one week you would probably be quartered; that is, you would not be let in till breakfast time, and your wage would be docked 3d or 4d. I was only pennied once but I had several near misses.

We did some talking on the way home that night. We realised it was going to be all sleep and work, but khaki and blue cloth was wanted quickly; the lads had to be properly dressed to go out to fight. But that night I determined I would not spend the rest of my life in the mill.

The overtime came and soon we were all wishing it would end. We got home at 8.00. We were too tired to go out and play, so sometimes we would just sit on the doorstep and talk, or read while thc light was good enough. At 9.30 it was time to get supper and go to bed. We carried on like this for about eight weeks, all through the warm weather of June and July. Our holiday week started the first Monday after 12 August and we were all looking forward to it. At last the great day arrived.

Chapter 7

A Holiday at Weel

I was going to stay for a week with my grandparents, who lived at Weel near Beverley. I had never been to stay with them, and was excited about going to the country, and especially to Beverley, wondering what I should remember of it; but after all there is not much you can remember of a place you left at the age of three.

I wore the new costume I had got at Whitsuntide, and felt very smart as I went to the railway station. I had been told all about having to change at Hull. I had a pound tucked away in an inside pocket, and a few shillings in my purse in case I wanted anything on the way. My elder sister saw me off. It was a lovely day. At Hull I enquired about the next train to Beverley and managed to change alright. My grandfather was meeting me at Beverley station.

When I got out of the train, I looked around. There were not many people in the station. I saw a typical farmer coming towards me. I was sure this must be my grandad. He took one look at me and said, "You must be Herbert's lass; well, get your bags together — we've got to call for your grandma and it won't do to keep her waiting". I followed him out of the station to where there was a horse and trap waiting. "Get in", he said, "and we'll be off. Whoa Nancy! Just od on a minute! We've got toon folk wi' us and they doan't knaw hoo to get in a trap; they're more used to these new-fangled trams. Noo that's better" — as I managed to pull myself up and get seated. "Noo we'll be off!" And with a flick of the reins away we went. The horse didn't seem to need any guiding, and we went down two or three streets to a small terrace house. "You'd better get down and come in; Mrs. Smith is sure to want to see you." I got down. He just told Nancy to stand still, then went and gave a loud knock, opening the door at the same time and calling out, "Ae you got your tea drinking done? I've somebody here to see you".

Inside my grandmother and Mrs. Smith were sitting at a table. They had finished their tea. I went over to grandma and kissed her and asked how she was. Then I said "hello" to Mrs. Smith, who asked who I was, and was I the sixth or the seventh? They both looked at me and wondered who I was like, deciding I had a look of my father round the mouth, but I had my mother's colouring. I wasn't really a Lount; I wasn't fair enough for one, although there had been one or two with more of a brunette colour. They had quite a discussion, until my grandad broke in with "Well, are you going to sit there all day yapping? Because I've summat else to do beside talk of noses and colour." At this my grandma got up and said she was ready. She was very straight. She was dressed all in black; her coat, which was of thin lacy material, was three-quarter length, and her skirts were very full and reached the ground. She had a bouquet of violets pinned in her coat, which I found out later were artificial. Her hair was white, and she wore a black bonnet with a big bow of ribbon at the side. She wore boots.

We went out and climbed into the trap. My grandad flicked the reins, said "get on wi' yer", and off we went. I sat at the back. As we trundled on my grandad called out, "We'll soon be going over t'river, so you'd better sit still or you might get a ducking". We crossed the river Hull by a wooden ferry bridge. "You'll see some ships being made here; some of the finest in the world". The shipyard was very busy and noisy. We then cantered along the country lane by the riverside, for about a mile and a half, when we turned in at the open gate of a farm yard. We drove right up to the back door, where my cousin Lottie was waiting. Grandma turned to Lottie and said, "Help your Grandad in with those things; then we'll have our tea". My grandma led me through the back kitchen, where there was a cheerful fire glowing on a well polished grate, to "the room".

This was a huge place and everything about it was well polished and dusted. At one end was a huge fireplace; brass fire irons and fender twinkled in the light from the fire. The floor was of red brick, but was almost covered by a carpet. In the centre was a large table, covered now with a red velvet cloth. Down one side was a large dresser or sideboard, with three mats on it, woven in bright wool. On the middle one stood a writing box, which when opened was like a desk, complete with pen, ink and writing paper. On the others stood a work-box and a button box. At the far end of the room was a piece of furniture matching the dresser, a cupboard resting on three drawers. Opposite the dresser was a side-table under the window with a plant on it. There were chairs at each side of the dresser, the cupboard, and the side-table. Two easy chairs were drawn up to the tabbed rug which was down in front of the fire. There was a grandfather clock in the far corner, near a door which led to the garden. It looked lovely to me. I stood on the rug and looked up

Maggie's grandparents, and a farm servant at Weel
(Photo courtesy of Margaret Walter)

at the mantelpiece; there was a china figure at each end, depicting War and
Peace, and one or two more little ornaments.

My grandma took her bonnet and coat off, and said to me, "You'd
better get out of that costume before we have our tea. Lottie'll show
you where to go." Just then Lottie came in and said, "Come on we'll go
upstairs". She led me through to the hall. This was really great; broad
stairs led up to the next floor. They were beautifully carpeted, as was
the hall. In the hall were three stands with stuffed animals in glass cases:
an owl, who looked very alive to me, a young fox, and some birds. The
stairs were in two flights. Hung on the wall over the first flight was a
text which I read every time I went up or down:

> Christ is the head of this house.
> The unseen guest at every meal.
> The silent listener to every conversation.

It made me think, but it seemed to me a bit sneaky. We went on a corridor
and to the room at the end. This was really smart. There was a huge four-
poster bed with curtains. I don't know how many feather mattresses it
had; when you got in you just sank into it. Lottie left me to get

changed. I looked all round the bedroom. There was a high chest of drawers and a wash-hand-stand with a china bowl, a jug of water, a soap-dish with some scented soap, and a tooth-brush container. There was a matching dressing table with two drawers and a mirror draped with curtaining which was tied back at each side with ribbon. Pinned to this at one side was a hair-tidy, very nicely embroidered, for putting the combings from your hair in. On the table was a brush and comb and two lovely little boxes decorated with sea shells. I hurriedly changed and went downstairs, making no sound on the thick carpet.

My grandma was sitting in a rocking chair, and Lottie was getting the table ready for tea. My grandad came in and we sat down to the meal; I was ready for it, having had nothing to eat since leaving Bradford at about 10 o'clock. Lottie brought in a piece of boiled bacon, and we had bread and butter, jam, and cakes. I was still a bit shy about talking. After tea I helped Lottie to clear away and wash up. She was about five years older than me; she would be about eighteen years old. I thought she was very nice looking; she had fair silky hair that came down to her waist when she took the pins out. I learned afterwards that grandma was very proud of Lottie's hair, and insisted on her brushing it for ten minutes every night. When the washing up was done she had to wash out the milk churns; then she said she would take me to see Uncle Arthur.

Uncle Arthur and Aunt Nellie lived across the road in the middle one of three cottages built on a little rise. They were very kind, and asked me if I had come to meet my cousins: Albert, about my age, Bella, a few years younger, and Arthur, about seven. We stayed a few minutes and then went for a walk round the village. This did not take long; there were only two other farms, the three cottages, a very small Methodist Chapel, and a public house. I think the pub was called the "Ferry Inn"; it was near the river, and there was a ferry to take you to the villages of Warne and Woodmansey. On the river bank we were joined by Bella and Arthur and some more boys and girls from the village. The boys started fishing. Lottie left me, saying she had some jobs to do, but Bella said she would be off to see her boyfriend. We sat on the river bank and talked. They were interested to hear about Bradford and the mill, and I was quite content to sit there, until one of the boys came and showed us his catch. He had a tin as big as a frying pan full of squirming eels. I ran away with the other girls and the boys chased us. Eventually we all sat on the bank again, and a boy started playing some popular songs on his mouth-organ: "It's a long way to Tipperary", "Keep the home fires burning", "Sister Susie's sewing shirts for soldiers". We all joined in the singing till the sun went down. When I got back to the farm grandma was combing her hair before going to bed; she told me to go down to the pantry and get what I wanted for supper. I got a piece of curd tart and a glass of milk. Then I said "goodnight" and went to sample that lovely bed.

The following day was a Sunday. After breakfast we made the beds; bed-making was really an art here. The bedclothes were all pulled back when we got up in the morning, and the beds left to cool or air. Now the pillows were taken off and given a good shake. The feather mattress was shaken from the sides and the corners, so that the feathers were shaken to the middle; then it was shaken again and patted with the hands till it was more or less level. Then the bed clothes were put on again. The result was that you felt as if you were sleeping on a cloud. Lottie said grandma insisted on this routine and would know instantly if the job was scamped. We had feather beds at home but we didn't make quite such a ritual of bed-making as this. In the afternoon we went to Sunday School. There were, I think, twelve pews and twelve scholars of all ages. Lottie played the organ. We had a layman to speak to us; he spoke again in the evening, when there were perhaps ten adults present.

Bella told me it was the Sunday School trip on Tuesday, and they were going to Hornsea. I wondered if I could go. She said of course I could; everybody went. On Monday the rully was got ready; seats from the Sunday School were fastened on. But I gathered there was some concern about who was going to drive. The weather was fine, and what men were left in the village were wanted for work in the fields. I was awakened the following morning to the sound of milk cans being rolled around. This happened every morning around 6 o'clock; the cans were filled, put in the trap, and taken to Beverley station to be taken on the Hull train. After breakfast we went out to see what kind of day it was going to be; most people thought it was going to be fine and very hot. Lottie could not be spared and I was to go with my other cousins. I was excited because I had never seen the sea. I went upstairs and got my purse; I intended to be one of the great spenders; grandma had given me sixpence, saying that would be quite enough to waste on the swings, but I slipped another two shillings in my purse.

About 8 o'clock we were told to climb on the wagon. Soon it was full; there were about thirty women and children, and I think only two men beside the driver. He I discovered was a cousin George of mine, who lived at Beverley and had reached home on leave from France that morning. On hearing that they were short of a driver for Weel Sunday School treat he had had a few hours' sleep and cycled over to offer his services. The two horses looked great in their red and blue braid, with their brasses shining. As we started off we were reasonably quiet, except for the mothers telling us to stop fidgetting and keep still or we might get thrown off. Then they would wonder if they had done right to come without raincoats, and others would say they always took theirs, "because yer niver knaw".

When we got to Beverley we started singing. We wanted everyone out to look at us and we certainly got a lot. They came running to their doors to wave and call out friendly greetings: "Hev a good day! Bring us some rock back!" I was busy looking around; when I spotted what I was looking for I yelled out to Bella, "That's it! That's where I was born!" Everyone else looked and I was glad the house looked clean and smart. We quietened down a bit after leaving Beverley, but when we got to Tickton and the other villages on the Hornsea road we burst into song. Villagers came to their doors and waved and laughingly told us we'd better go back, it was raining at Hornsea; but they couldn't dampen our spirits - this was our day.

Eventually we reached the sea front at Hornsea. George said he was going onto the sand for a sleep. We got our buckets and spades and started to play; the grown-ups just sat around watching. It wasn't long before shoes and stockings were off, but we were warned to keep on the edge of the water and not venture far in. I thought this was grand. We pulled our skirts up and tucked them in our knickers, then ran and splashed for all we were worth. The sea looked lovely, blue and silver. Then we spotted the swing-boats and off we went for a ride. There was not a big demand for them, so the man didn't stop us till we were called for dinner. We pulled hard and tried to make the boat go over the top, in competition with each other, standing up in our enthusiasm until our parents shouted and told us to sit down before we broke our necks. But we all landed safely, ready for the sandwiches which had been brought on the rully. We got tea at Baker's eating house, and were allowed to sit at their outside tables.

After dinner we were told to sit down and let our dinners settle. We did, for about ten minutes. Then we made more sand castles, went and splashed in the sea again, and had another go on the swing-boats. Some of us older ones thought it would be nice if we could go for a walk and look at the shops; we thought we were too big to be with the children all the time. So we asked permission and were told, "Ay, get off wi' yer, but don't be away long, and keep together and don't get lost". Off we went. We bought plums, which we ate, and then we vied with each other as to who could spit the stone farthest. We looked in all the gift shops and bought a few small presents. I bought a little ornament with the Hornsea coat of arms for sixpence, some sticks of rock, and some sweets to eat on the journey home. I still had a penny left for another turn on the swings.

After that we ran splashing in the water again as the tide came up, and were constantly warned by the grown-ups not to go too far. Some of us wanted to go for a ride on the donkeys - about four had lined up a little way off. We had all "spent up", but someone paid for us. I was a bit scared because I had never been on a donkey before. My donkey just walked and no coaxing would get a trot out of him until we turned for home and he suddenly broke into a gallop. It took me all my time to hold on and everyone laughed at my undignified appearance. Soon afterwards it was tea time; more sandwiches and cakes were brought out, the women wondering all the time where we put it all and vowing once a year was enough to bring bairns to Hornsea. But they themselves did full justice to the good things on the tables and made good-humoured criticisms of each other's baking.

Now the older ones wanted to be starting back. Some of them were saying there was thunder about, though I wondered how they knew when it was such a perfect day — hot sun, hardly any breeze, blue skies with, yes, just a little black cloud, but thunder, no. It was nearly 6 o'clock when the rully was brought round and we were told to climb on. We were still in good spirits; the day wasn't over yet, we still had the journey home, and we would sing and fetch everyone out as we passed through the villages. At the first few villages the children came out and asked if we had any rock. The women were prepared for this and threw a few sticks of rock to them, shouting "share that among you". The men would call, "You'd better hurry, it's going to rain", and indeed it did begin to look a bit black, but we would not believe it was going to rain. Then came the first roll of thunder. Those of us who had brought them started buttoning our coats. Then the rain came, big drops, faster and faster. We were more than half way home but by the time we reached Tickton we were all wet through. The lady sitting next to me had a baby whose clothes were wet through; she took them off and I wrung them out over the side of the rully. One of the men took his jacket off — it was still dry as he had an old sack over his shoulders — and they wrapped the baby in it. We jogged on, and by the time we reached Weel we were all soaked to the skin. My grandma gave me a drink of milk well laced with whisky. I went straight to bed, slept till nearly noon the next day, and was none the worse for the wetting.

On the Thursday grandad was going to Beverley and I was told I could go with him, visit two aunts I had there, and have a walk round the shops to buy presents. I first called on my Aunt Nellie, my father's sister, who lived at the bottom of Norwood Grove. She was very busy but she gave me some lemonade and cake. One of my cousins showed me my uncle's collection of butterflies, beautiful specimens all neatly mounted in two large glass cases. Then I said I must go, as my Aunt Charlotte was expecting me to dinner. Aunt Charlotte, my mother's sister, lived at Hull Bridge, and there I met my Uncle George and my cousin Mabel. After dinner we had a pleasant time looking through postcard and photo albums. Then I went into Beverley. I went to see St. Mary's Church, where my parents were married, a beautiful building. I went a little way up North Bar Without; it was very quiet and pleasant there, with no sound except the cawing of crows and now and again a horse and trap going by. I thought I would like to live there. Then I went to the Saturday Market, had a look at the market cross, and bought my presents: a little ornament for grandma, a tin of his favourite sweets for grandad, chocolate for Lottie, trinkets for friends at home, sticks of rock for the family, and one of those lovely shell boxes for myself. My £1 was beginning to look very small, but I was enjoying myself. Finally I went and had a look at the Minster. I went inside and wandered round. I didn't understand architecture but I could recognise beauty, and it really is one of the most beautiful cathedrals I have ever seen.

I had to meet my grandad outside the station at 4.30, and I had learnt enough about him to know that if I was not there he would go without me, saying I was young enough to walk. I got there in good time and saw the trap, but waited until I saw my grandad before getting in. He came bustling out of the station saying "Come on wi' yer! I thowt yer wer niver coming! Here, help me in wi' these parcels. Whoa Nancy! yer want yer tea di yer? Well, yer mun wait." We got in and set off at a brisk trot. Grandad was very cheerful and said, "Well, have you had a good day? What did your aunties have to tell you?" I said I'd had a lovely day and had bought all my presents. "Presents? What d' yer want, spending yer money on such like rubbish? I get on very weel wi' oot presents." I said I had bought one for him, and showed him the tin of sweets. He was pleased with them, though he kept telling me I should "niver have any money as long as I spent it on suchlike rubbish".

We arrived home in time for tea. Grandma came out, looked at grandad, and said, "You've been calling at the Station Hotel, I see". "Just one," he said, "just to slek dust". I had quite a lot to tell grandma. She wanted to know how everyone was, what I'd been doing, and if I liked Beverley. I gave her and Lottie their presents. After tea I went across to meet Bella, and we spent the evening on the river bank again with the other boys and girls, talking and singing popular songs. The next day I overheard grandma giving grandad what she would call a "dressing down". I got the story from Lottie later. It seemed the previous night grandad had got up after tea, saying he would just have a walk round. He liked a drink of beer, and had brought a couple of bottles home with him, but beer wasn't allowed in the house and he knew that however carefully he hid it, it would be found. So he went to the trap, got the bottles, and hid them in a patch of nettles at the bottom of the front garden. Feeling pleased with himself, he started whistling as he walked away, and that was his undoing. Grandma heard the whistling and went to the window to see what was going on. She saw grandad at the bottom of the garden and was sure he was up to something, so she waited till he had gone to bed and then had a walk down the garden. Her sharp eyes saw where the nettles had been disturbed and soon she was marching back to the house with the bottles. The following morning after breakfast grandad took a stroll in the garden. This time he didn't come away whistling; as grandma would have said she gave him the length of her tongue, and the beer was emptied down the drain. Lottie said this wasn't the first time. Once she had found two bottles in the copper in the wash house; they were of course confiscated but grandad kept on trying. He became quite a character, and it was well known that on market days he would go for some refreshment and the horse would take him home. He would get in the trap, give the horse a flick, and with a "Home nancy!" they would set off. Before long grandad would begin to nod, the reins would go slack, and the horse would go trotting on. It turned in at the gate, which was always open, and pulled up at the stalls, where it would be chewing hay when grandad woke up with a start some time later.

Friday was a very hot day. Bella and I went down to the fields and took lunch to the men. We dawdled about and the whirr of the reaper almost sent us to sleep. It was almost teatime when we got back. I went upstairs and packed my case. In the evening I said goodbye to the boys and girls I met on the river bank. We laughed and joked. Bella teased me, saying I should have to kiss them all goodbye. This I refused to do, but one of the boys, a bit more daring than the rest, grabbed hold of me and kissed me. I was so astounded I brought my hand up and smacked his face, but we all parted good friends. They all seemed to think I was lucky to live in Bradford; and I would have been quite happy to have stayed in Weel and lived their happy carefree life. But I was to leave in the morning. This had been my first holiday and I had enjoyed almost every minute of it.

Morning came, and grandad was ready with the trap to take me into Beverley. I said goodbye to grandma and cousin Lottie, thanking them for a really lovely holiday. Grandad put my case in the trap and said, "You'd better be sharp and get in me lass, or you'll be walking". It was a fine morning. As we jogged along the road the river could hardly be seen on account of the high rushes growing on the bank. Before long the twin towers of the minster came into view, gleaming in the sun. Then we heard the noise of the shipyard as we neared the bridge. Grandad had a word with the man on duty there. "So you're going home again, are you?" he said, turning to me; "I've no doubt you'll have spent up?" "Not quite," I said, "I'm going round the market before the train leaves". "Aye, theer yer go; it'll burn a hole in yer pocket if yer doan't spend it". "Well, we mun be off", said grandad. He had to go to the station, where I said goodbye and thank you. I left my case in the luggage office, and went into the town.

In the market there were all kinds of stalls, but such a lot selling butter! This was made by the local farmers, and each pat of butter had a pattern marked on. There was bacon in huge sides; beef; pork pies; and sausages. All kinds of confectionary; lots of home-baked scones, pies, curd tarts and tea cakes. There were greengrocery stalls, gardening stalls, clothes stalls, and gift stalls. Here you could buy pretty purses and little china ornaments, all with the Beverley crest on them. The time soon passed. I had tea and cakes in a cafe, and then went back to the station. Grandad had finished his business and come to see me off; there was the trap, and there he was, talking to a porter. I got my luggage and joined them. Grandad said: "Well, have you spent up? Got a load of rubbish, I'll be bound. Here's a few goodies for you; you'll not get any like them in Bradford I know. Well, train's just coming in, so we'll away and let you get on." And with that he was off, and I was left to get on the train.

Which I did; but with a heavy heart. I didn't want to go back to Bradford and a life in the mill. I wanted to stay here, but I knew that couldn't be. I found a seat, took out a book I had got in the market, had one of grandad's goodies, and prepared to make the best of the journey. I spent most of it looking out of the window; my own thoughts were company enough. Why had we had to leave Kirk Hammerton? I might have been going home there now, instead of to Bradford and the mill. Then I realised I was fourteen now, and had we still been at Kirk Hammerton I should have been looking for a place, that is, going into service. Oh well, that wouldn't be so bad; but the mill girls looked down on domestic servants and referred to them as skivvies. Well, I would join the night school in September; I would go in for typing and shorthand, then I would be able to get a job in an office. In the meantime I would get books out of the library and read up a bit on these subjects.

The train arrived at Forster Square station in the early evening. I looked up and down the platform to see if there was anyone to meet me. I saw Nellie waiting by the barrier, and it felt grand to be home. She said everyone was well; my mother had been worrying about whether I would make the right change at Leeds and remember to save twopence for my tram fare. Feeling very grown-up I said of course I had; as a matter of fact I had nearly four shillings left, and I would treat them all to fish and chips for supper. When I got home my tea was ready. Everyone else had finished theirs and they all started asking questions. Had I behaved myself? Had I been to see all my aunties? How was everyone? Did I like Weel? Had I been to the Minster? I talked and talked while I wired into great chunks of bread and jam and home-made teacakes. Then I wanted to know about their holiday. My mother and father just sat back and listened while we talked our heads off. We exchanged presents. At last my mother said it was time for bed for all of us.

The following day, Sunday, I went for a walk with my friend Edith to Chellow Dene. On a fine day in late August the woods on each side of the reservoirs were glorious, with their different shades of green and brown. Edith had not been away for the holidays and was interested to hear all about mine. I told her how I wanted to get out of the mill, and she said she was quite happy at the box works, but the wage was poor. We came to the conclusion that we would wait and see what we could do at evening classes.

Chapter 8

Back to Work

The following morning I was up at ten to six and back at the mill. It was nice to see everyone again, but, oh! the day seemed endless, and we noticed as we came home that the days were shortening. On the dark evenings we were glad to stay in and help with the ironing, or read. It was soon time to enrol for night school. Edith changed her mind and did not go; I went, determined to go in for secretarial work of some kind. I knew now that what I really wanted to be was a teacher; I had told my parents, but I had now left school and they could not have afforded to keep me there anyway, so I settled for office work. But at my night school interview I was told I couldn't possibly take shorthand and typing, and was advised to go in for dressmaking, needlework and cookery, which I did. Three nights a week would thus be taken up. I was given a list of things I should need for each class, which looked pretty formidable to me, but my parents helped, and I was all set.

I enjoyed the classes. I found it interesting draughting patterns to fit myself, and made a blouse and a summer dress at the dressmaking class, which I had a lot of pleasure in wearing. The teacher was very patient, and as there were about 25 in the class she needed to be. The needlework class was fine too; we made a sampler using different stitches, and we could talk as we worked, so the evening passed pleasantly. I was not so pleased with the cookery class; it seemed to me a waste of time to make such small quantities as we made, and mine was usually eaten as soon as I had shown it to my mother on arriving home. The winter passed and I realised I was not going to be a dressmaker at the end of it. I received a lovely brush and comb set at the end of the year as a prize for good attendance, and a free pass for the following year.

Work, night school, the Band of Hope meetings on Saturday nights, Sunday School and walks on Sunday; this then was the pattern of my life. Meanwhile the war, which everyone had said was going to be over in three months' time, had been going on for over a year. It was beginning to touch us. One day at work I was told of the death of a boy from Lupton

Street; his mother was given the official letter, and just ran out screaming and collapsed in the road. The shooting of Nurse Cavell was talked about in the mills and everyone was horrified. We heard too of the Zeppelin raids; one over Scarborough sounded much too near for our peace of mind. The boys who came home on leave wanted to do anything but talk of the war, but every day we were hearing of young men going to join the forces; it seemed the army couldn't get enough. Posters stared at you from all the hoardings; Kitchener's famous one, "Your Country Needs You", must have been the means of sending many boys to their deaths. My brother George tried to enlist, but was turned down on account of his eyesight. Food was getting scarce, and when a shop had a delivery of butter, margarine, sugar or tea the word soon got round and long queues were formed. Butter was sold in two or four ounce quantities. It was hard on people with families who were unable to spare the time to queue, and we found ourselves going round town on Saturday afternoons, joining any queue, just to get something. We were exhorted to "eat more potatoes" and "dig for victory", so all the allotments were producing their utmost, tended mainly by the older men and the women. Some of the work in the mills previously done by men was now being done by women, and they were also being used as conductresses on the trams and as cleaners on the railway. Still I went to the mill, still wishing I could do something different. We were really needed there, so we had a rise in wages.

The summer came and we started going to our local swimming bath. If we hurried after leaving work and arrived before 6 p.m. we could get in for twopence, so once a week we ran up to Drummond Road baths and splashed around. I couldn't swim. Although there were swimming periods for schoolchildren, I was not in a swimming class till my last year, and then we never got round to getting me a swimming costume before I left.

That summer we had a family holiday at Bridlington. It was a great occasion, and a most enjoyable holiday. It was the thing in those days to get up at 6.30 a.m. and go down to the sea for a dip. The joys of early morning bathing can be overrated; however warm the morning, the sea was cold, and there was much screaming and shouting till we all got wet. Then after a good rub down we ran back to the digs, and crept into bed again till breakfast time. There was of course no sunbathing, and if you wanted to go bathing or swimming you hired a tent. You selected your spot and pegged it out, and then any number could get changed in it. The idea of course was to have your tent as near the sea as possible. There was many a hurried scramble to get your clothes on

The Drummond Road Baths, Manningham
(Source: City of Bradford *Bradford Public Baths*, 1905)

again after bathing if the tide happened to be coming in. Once we had all
been in the water and got dressed again except my eldest sister Bella, and
her friend, Liz. They were really enjoying themselves, and although the
tide was coming in they stayed till the last minute; the sea was almost to
the tent when they scrambled in. We were all sitting further back, laughing at them, when we saw a pair of corsets floating away on the waves. A
big wave had come right into the tent. Bella and Liz retrieved their clothes
while the rest of us hastily took the tent down.

Bridlington was a wonderful place in those days and we spent many
happy holidays there. We always stayed at the North end, and always
had a walk on to Sewerby, sometimes going further, to Danes' Dyke
and Flamborough. On a sunny day this was a lovely walk, the sea at
one side, the cornfields at the other. There were no buildings then. We
also used to go on the pier, watching the fishing and of course we had
to have a sail in the *Yorkshireman*. This was one of the highlights of a
Bridlington holiday. It was a paddle-steamer, and for a shilling you
went out for a sail lasting about two hours, round Flamborough Head.
It was grand to sit and do nothing and feel the sea spray on your face,
and get a great appetite for tea. There was also a singing booth at the

top of the pier. Here the popular songs of the day were played on a piano, we joined in the singing, and the owner of the booth sold copies of the songs and music at a penny each. It was the thing to take a few copies home, and it was a grand place to spend a wet afternoon. Other entertainments included watching a one-armed man who made a living by drawing on the sand. He had a huge piece of the beach, which he flattened out, and then he would draw pictures, mostly of churches, and you threw coppers into his cap. There was another man who used to do tricks in the water, when the tide was up. He would dive in from the pier, and then imitate a porpoise, a seal, or a spinning top. I was fascinated, and made up my mind I would swim; much later I accomplished all the tricks I saw him do. All this and sitting on the sands in a deckchair, reading or crocheting, was holidaying at Bridlington from about 1915 to 1920.

I went to evening classes again. This time I took courses in dressmaking, first-aid and swimming. My sister Annie came with me to the dressmaking class, but she wouldn't go to the others. The dressmaking and first-aid classes were held in a very comfortable room at the Y.W.C.A., with big easy chairs and a nice carpet. On the first-aid night we had great fun bandaging each other up, and at the end of the year I took a certificate in this subject. The swimming class was my favourite. Green Lane School bath is still just as it was then, except of course that the water is now chlorinated; in those days it used to be changed twice a week. Miss Greenwood, who taught us, was very dedicated. It was funny to be addressed as "Miss" by her, but it helped us to think of ourselves as young ladies. She showed us how to do the strokes, and then we got into the water. You were given a rope with a noose, which you put round your waist, and then from about half-way across the bath you launched yourself on the water, trying to use your arms and legs as you had been shown, while she pulled you in. You just kept trying till you got confidence, and with a few duckings your efforts were rewarded and you could swim. I shall never forget the thrill when I heard Miss Greenwood say, "You're swimming! Keep it up!" By the end of the year I was swimming in the deep end and enjoying every minute of it.

On Saturday afternoons we would go to the cinema. Cowboy pictures were the favourites, and we were just as fond of horror pictures as children today are. Sex had not invaded the films and we booed and stamped if a kiss lasted more than three or four seconds. Our favourite heroines were Mary Pickford and Pearl White. We loved the comics, Fatty Arbuckle, Charlie Chaplin and Harold Lloyd.

War went on, but the glory had all gone. We heard horrible stories from the soldiers, and read them in the newspapers. The evening paper now had almost every night a column of names of boys killed or missing. The "Bradford Pals" had their headquarters in the old skating rink on Manningham Lane (now the Mecca Ballroom) and kept sending lads abroad; nearly all of them were killed on the Somme in July 1916. The recruiting posters still drew men in, and the authorities were not so choosy as they had been the previous year. My brother George pestered the recruiting centres in Bradford, Leeds and Halifax, but they kept turning him down. Yet I don't remember his having a day's illness till he did finally get in, in 1918, and then he spent a large part of his time in hospital.

Things were different at home now. My elder sisters, Elizabeth and Nellie, got jobs as conductresses on the trams. Bella left service, came home, and joined them. So we never seemed to be quiet; with three conductresses and Charlie on the railway all working different turns there was always someone coming or going, and my mother was always preparing meals. I was not unhappy but I still wanted to get out of the mill. My sister Annie joined the Land Army, and I tried to join too. My friend and I went to the recruiting office at Leeds and said we were eighteen, but when our papers were sent to our parents they gave our real ages, so we were not accepted. When I got my first-aid certificate I decided to become a nurse, but was told at both the Bradford and the Halifax hospitals to come back when I was eighteen. I was depressed; it seemed you could do nothing till you were eighteen. But I did join the St. John's Ambulance Brigade.

I now decided I would go into service. My friends thought I was mad; to be a "skivvy" was to be the lowest of the low. My sisters also tried to talk me out of it, giving me the benefit of their experience, but I had made up my mind. My mother agreed to let me try it, feeling sure a month would be enough for me. I took a position with three sisters, schoolteachers, at 16s. a month and my keep. I was to have one night out a week and alternate Saturday and Sunday afternoons and evenings, the usual arrangement. I had to have three morning dresses and aprons, two black afternoon dresses and aprons, and a cap. Luckily my sisters had finished with their service uniforms, which were altered to fit me, and I thought I looked very smart in them. The three sisters lived in one of a row of bay-windowed terrace houses in Laisteridge Lane, and I went there about August 1916.

One of the ladies, Miss Mabel, as I was told to address her, stayed at home to manage the house; Miss Maud was a schoolteacher; Miss Annie was in a hospital. I had to get up at 7 a.m., make a fire in the dining room, go round with the sweeper and duster, and make breakfast. The ladies came down at 8 to 8.15. After breakfast I washed up and helped with the household chores. On Mondays we would wash clothes in the cellar.

In those days it was quite a business, but I knew it all because I had helped my mother, who followed the same routine. First the clothes were sorted into whites, coloureds, woollens, dirty dusters and so on. The whites were washed by hand in the tub on the sink, or given a good possing in the peggy-tub. Next they were boiled, rinsed, and if necessary starched with dolly-blue. Then they were folded and put through the wringer, a big one with wooden rollers turned by hand, and finally they were hung out to dry. The coloureds were dealt with in the same way, except that they were not boiled. It was quite a tiring day; the cellar opened onto the back yard, but there were five steps up and down every time you hung anything out. When the washing was done the tubs were washed out, the mangle was fastened down, the floor washed, and everything put away. After tea sometimes we would do the ironing, and sometimes it was left till Tuesday morning.

Miss Mabel went out to do the shopping and queuing, so I was often alone during the day, and I liked the freedom of being left to get on with my work. I had quite a big and nicely furnished attic room, where I did a lot of reading in the evenings, borrowing books from my employers. But I very much missed the company of my family and people my own age, and I did wish I could go out. On my days off I walked home, or to concerts and services at the Eastbrook Mission, but I missed my walks in the country. And I realised very soon that 16s. a month wasn't going to go very far.

Then one day when we had an extra big wash, which lasted past our usual lunch time, I was tired and asked if we couldn't break off and have our lunch, which was ready and only spoiling. Miss Maud was helping me — it must have been a school holiday — and she said, "If you want yours go get it; I'm going to finish down here". So I went up for my lunch. I would have been quite happy to have gone on with the work afterwards, but Miss Maud came up and said she'd finished and she thought she'd earned my wages that day. I was astounded and hurt, and replied that if she thought so, she could have them and a month's notice. The next day she apologised, but I had determined to go. I think really I was homesick.

Now I had to think about another job. I certainly did not want to go back into the spinning, but I could not afford to be out of work. My friend Edith told me she had heard they were wanting girls in the warehouse at Lister's Mill, and it was nice clean work. She and I were interviewed and told we could start straight away; the pay was 11s. a week. I was given a job of stacking large bobbins of cotton, in the order of their colours, on shelves. I was in a room where the girls had machines for running sewing cotton from these bobbins onto reels, which were then sent to the packers, who stuck labels on and packed them into boxes, ready to be sent to the wholesalers. Like everything new it was very interesting at first. The large bobbins came up to me in skeps. I never knew there were so many colours; there must have been about 300. I had to be careful to keep them all in their proper places. The girls on the machines were on piece-work, at which they could earn 16 or 17s. a week, so they didn't want to lose any time. They came to me with their orders; my shelves were all the way round the room and reached the ceiling, so I had a ladder to move and run up and down for every order. I was fascinated by the packers; they would endlessly, and at great speed, take labels in their left hands, lick them, and stick them on reels with their right hands. A damp sponge was provided but most girls found it quicker to use their tongues.

Soon after starting at Lister's we got a rise, 12s 6d a week, but it still was not as much as the spinners were getting, and I did want a job where I could save. I had seen so much of people as they got older, with nothing at the back of them, having to go out charring or something, when they had enough to do to look after their own homes. Another reason for wanting to leave Lister's was that it was a long uphill walk from where I lived. We started at 6.30 a.m. and we had to allow half an hour for the walk on cold winter mornings. We could have got a bus, but we didn't believe in spending money on buses if we could walk. I stayed at Lister's for about five months during the winter of 1916–17. Before the winter was out I went to work in the twisting department at Smith's on City Road, which was nearer home and on the level. But as I passed Drummond's Mill on my way to work I often wished I was back there. That winter was very severe; we had snow drifts six feet high, but the cold was the worst and it took us all our time to keep warm. The mills were always warm, so there was no problem there. I hadn't time to come home for dinner, so both breakfast and dinner were packed up for me. At Smith's I remember there was a girl about my age who was a lovely singer, and sometimes she would sing for us during the meal break. She worked near me and I could hear her singing while she worked. I was no singer myself, though I sang all the popular songs of the day while working, as we all did: "Tipperary", "I'm forever blowing bubbles", "Sister Susie", and

> K-k-k-Katie, beautiful Katie!
> You're the only g-g-g-girl that I adore!
> And when the m-moon shines, on the c-cowshed,
> I'll be waiting by the k-k-k-kitchen door!

After a month or two at Smith's I heard Drummond's wanted some twisters, so I went back there. The twisting department was considered "one up" on the spinning, though really the process was very similar, winding the yarn from one bobbin to another.

It was about this time that my sister Elizabeth, who had been courting for some time, told us they had decided to get married. This was a great event and we were all greatly excited. Her husband-to-be had been stationed at Bradford Moor barracks with the R.A.S.C. He was on his last leave before being sent overseas, so the wedding was hurried forward and they were married at St Jude's Church on 15th February 1917. Bessie continued to live at home and work on the trams. That way they could save up towards buying a home when the war was over. Though weddings were not the big affairs then that they are now, we had quite a celebration. My mother made the wedding cake, and after the ceremony everyone came home to a very good tea. There were two or three sittings down; all our family, a few friends and one or two cousins came. Although the food shortage was almost desperate by this time, with the help of a little here and there a real good wedding feast was put on and everyone enjoyed themselves. I had set my heart on buying Bessie a lustre flower vase; it was 7s 6d., a really vast amount of money in those days. I saw it in the shop opposite Drummond's every day for weeks before I had saved up the 7s 6d. Then I went in and bought it. Bessie and Walt were as pleased with it as I was, and it had a place of its own in the centre of their sideboard for many years. I once read that only the poor know the real joy of giving, and I do know that when you deny yourself to give, then you get a great deal of pleasure.

I had stopped going to Sunday School and for a time I didn't belong anywhere. I used to go to Eastbrook Mission on Sunday nights with my sister Annie. At this time Mr Gilbert Muir was the pastor there. He was a fiery evangelical and was very popular with his congregation. The evening services were always full, and often there were people sitting on the steps and the window bottoms. The hall seated about two thousand people and was the centre of much religious activity. The Brotherhood had about two thousand members; almost every man you met in Bradford belonged to it. They wore a blue and gold badge of clasped hands and the letters EB underneath. Now the war was thinning the ranks and although the numbers were still strong they were mainly older men, and one began to wonder who would be there when these passed on. Open air meetings were held three nights a week, and Annie and I often attended them. We also enjoyed the concerts, which usually consisted of a quartet of singers and an entertainer, sometimes a magician or a story-teller, occasionally a piano soloist; and the price was only 2d.

I was growing up now and beginning to ask myself questions. I couldn't

"I used to to to Eastbrook Mission on Sunday nights ... At this time Mr Gilbert Muir was the pastor there." Note the Rev. G. Gilbert Muir's name on the placards in this photograph from the Pratt Collection in Bradford's Central Library. (Photo by Christopher Pratt, published courtesy of David W. Pratt)

reconcile myself to the idea that a just and loving God intended that half his children should live on a starvation diet, while others lived in mansions and could employ a horde or servants to do for them. I was always deeply religious, but I was unable to talk about religious subjects. I believed in my God as I had been taught to do from childhood, and I had a great belief in the power of prayer. I continued to go to Eastbrook services till Annie started courting and I was not keen to play gooseberry. A friend asked me to go to Salem Sunday School with her. I joined the young ladies' class there and continued to go till I got married in 1937. Miss Ackroyd, our leader, was a very dedicated person and was very well liked by all of us.

Food was getting to be quite a problem, and some things were rationed, though general rationing was not introduced till later. We were short of everything and a loaf of bread went up to 9d. We used to get some horrible black looking beans which were supposed to be very good for us; at least they took the edge off our appetites. We were encouraged to eat more lentils, so we had soups of beans and lentils. However much we at home went short, the Government saw that the soldiers were well fed; they were fighting and dying for a shilling a day, so I suppose it was the least the Government could do, though when they got to the front line it was mostly corned beef and biscuits. At this time in the mill we heard a lot about Russian workers uniting to overthrow their Government, and some of us thought it was quite a good idea. I think the workers all over the world were waking up to the injustices done to the working class. We mill workers had the evidence before our eyes of the mansions the millowners lived in, while we were always on the poverty line and one week from the workhouse, as the older ones put it. The workers were beginning to realise that the only way to better their lot was to unite. The miners' slogan of eight hour's work, eight hour's play, eight hour's sleep and eight bob a day was taken up by the dockers, and we in the mills began to think we ought to have a little more of this world's goods. We were always exhorted to be patriotic and back up the lads at the front. Conscription was introduced and men between nineteen and thirty were called up; men up to fifty years old were accepted. Everyone was very tired of the war. The Americans had now joined in on our side. This of course boosted morale but the wise ones said the war must surely be nearing its end or they wouldn't have entered. However they played a great part in our victory the following year. Several of the boys we had known had been killed, and now the glory had gone out of the war; it all seemed so senseless. We had all been thrilled earlier to see pictures of His Majesty King George V in the trenches, and the Prince of Wales marching with his battalion of the Grenadier Guards, but these things didn't bring back the lads nor end the war.

Despite everything we managed to live happily enough. We had our work and this took up a large part of our time. We were still working a 55½ hour week: 10 hours a day and 5½ Saturday mornings. In the evenings during this summer of 1917 we would have a stroll in the park. Then at the week-end there was the cinema, or a walk round the markets hoping to get something, or Eastbrook Hall concerts. On Sundays we went to Salem Sunday School, after which we would go for a long walk. We were fortunate in Bradford that we had such lovely walks within easy reach of a 2d tram ride; Cottingley, Hirst Woods, Shipley Glen. Lots of these walks are now gone; they have been built over.

It was about this time that Gipsy Smith the great evangelist came and held meetings at Eastbrook Hall every evening, for one week. My friend and I attended one of these, and at the close we went out with other converts to acknowledge the Lord Jesus as our Saviour. We were conducted into a large room and asked to sit down and wait for a counsellor to come and speak to us. But when we saw the clock turning 9.30 and nobody had been to us I said we had better go home. We were not allowed out after 10 p.m. and we hadn't our tram fares home, so we slipped quietly out. Going home Edith said she wondered what they would have said to us. I replied, 'I think they would have told us to obey the Commandments, and that's what I'm going to try to do'. So we both promised to try and be good Christians. We got home for 10 o'clock and I told my mother and father about the meeting. My mother said it wouldn't matter that I hadn't seen the counsellor, so long as I tried to live up to all that I'd promised.

Dancing had now become popular. We used to have dances at Sunday School, always in aid of something or other. Our class usually had the managing of these events. We didn't make a lot of profit but it gave us something to do. Dances then were not just free and easy jiving. We would draw up a programme of usually 18 to 24 dances, always beginning and ending with a waltz. The first half of the programme would read something like this: Waltz, Foxtrot, Valeta, Quickstep, Waltz, Valeta, Foxtrot, Lancers, Waltz, Supper. The second half would be similar to the first. Sometimes we would include a Tango, and always at least one Military Twostep. The supper was included in the price of admission, which was a shilling, and usually consisted of buns and biscuits. We had small printed programmes, with the names of the dances and spaces for partners' signatures, for which a little pencil was attached. We tried to get every dance booked, but if partners were few we danced with each other. The dances were usually from 7.30 till 10 o'clock. We continued with these dances for years after the war, in the time of the Charleston and Black Bottom. Fancy Dress dances were very popular and we had one or two of these. It was only when the dance was over, and you had to walk home, that you realised how tired you were. We had great fun and never missed a dance.

I still worked at Drummond's. My father, who had been Night Watchman there, was now the Time Office or pennyhoilman. He was in the office by the front gates, and any latecomers had to go through the office, leave their names and numbers with him, and have a penny knocked off their wage. The wages were better now and at home things were a little easier as we had more money coming in. I was still handing all my wages to my mother, who then gave me my spending money, which at a penny in the shilling now amounted to 2/-, or sometimes more. We were on piece work and our wages varied a little each week. However my mother thought it was time that we learned to handle our own money, so we, that is my younger sister and I, started doing as the older ones did, paying jock brass, that is paying a fixed amount for our food and paying for

"Time is Money"
My father was now the Time Office, or "Pennyhoilman"
(Photo courtesy Stroud Riley Drummond)

everything else ourselves. We paid 15/- a week jock brass, and with the ten or eleven left, we had to buy clothes, save for holidays and pay for our own amusements. We usually put aside 2/- a week for holidays; occasionally I would put 1/- or 6d in the Penny Bank, 'for when I grow old' I used to say. We always put away 2/- for new clothes. We still got a new outfit at Whitsuntide, which was expected to last till the next Whit. Shoes were the biggest problem, they seemed to wear out so quick, and were always wanting mending. We learned to mend our own. We always had a cobbler's last and my mother or father would often mend our shoes, so we did the same. My sister Bessie was the best at this, and I think she really enjoyed doing it, and later on, when she had her own young family, would sit in an evening, mending shoes. She did it better than her husband, who came from Dorset and had evidently not been brought up to fend for himself so much. Also if she was in a temper she would get the last out and a pair of shoes, and work it out.

There was still discontent in the mills, and now the workers were trying to get organised in order to get better conditions. Then the war, which had dragged on so long, at last came to an end. We had heard rumours for

1918 Armistice Celebrations in the weaving shed at Drummond's Mill.
Maggie's father is on the extreme right.
(Photo courtesy Margaret Walter)

weeks. There was revolution in Berlin we heard. Then on November 11, 1918, while at work, we heard that the war was really over. We went mad, machines were stopped, trimmings were brought out that were used for Christmas, and we started trimming our machines. We got together in groups and talked and talked. We sang all the popular songs, we danced and did anything but work. At last the engine stopped and the overlooker told us we could all go home; I think it was about the middle of the afternoon. Outside we all linked arms and singing and dancing we went home. After a hasty tea we went out. We had to do something, so we would make a bonfire. We collected old rubbish, took it to the centre of the street and lit it. Then we roasted potatoes in the hot ashes, and danced and sang round the fire. We went into town to see what was happening there. There were just crowds of people promming the streets and singing. We came back to the fire until we were brought in and told that war or no war we had to go to work in the morning and we'd better get off to bed. I think we thought that now we should not be making the hated khaki and blue we had been spinning so long, but no, it takes time to get back to normal and it was many more months before we saw the end of this.

In the months to come we were to learn something of what wars bring. We thought the boys were going to come home and everything would be normal, but no, my brother Charles, who had been called up on his 18th birthday in February 1918, was sent to India, and although the war was over the boys were still being kept in the army to do their time. The trains kept coming in with their loads of wounded men. Every week now there were flag days for one deserving cause or another. The unemployment rate kept going up, and food was short. The men coming home were amazed when they realised how little rations were, but still we survived and managed to get a certain amount of enjoyment out of life. Such is youth. I think it must have been much harder for the older ones.

I still wanted to leave the mill. I began to think I should be going there till I was old like Mrs Smith. I tried to save because I didn't want to finish up in the workhouse. My father used to advise me to settle down and be glad I had a job to go to, lots of people hadn't. Well the winter came and brought with it Asian Flu. It was like a plague. Almost every house had someone down with it, sometimes the whole family down with it. The key would be left outside, where the doctor knew where to get it. Almost everyone on our street had it, some it attacked worse than others. The after effects were very bad and most of us were unable to get the little luxuries that help in convalescence. The depression that followed was worse. However we got through that winter. My sister Nellie, who had been working on the trams, took it worst in our family. She had not been well for some time and had been to Bridlington for a change, which did seem to help for a while, but the cough persisted. She had left the trams and gone back to the mill, but nothing we could get for her seemed to cure the cough, and she was at home quite a lot, and when it was fine would wrap up and go into the park. Then one morning after the doctor and a specialist had been, I knew my mother was more upset than usual. He had told her it was tuberculosis. This was early 1919. We all did everything we could to make life pleasant for her, but in May 1919, Nellie died.

I had never come up against death before. It was just something that happened to other people, not our family; and Nellie was so lovely, fair hair, blue eyes and such a sweet nature. I remember the day she died. My mother sent me to go for the doctor. I hurried along Manningham Lane to Marlborough Road for our Dr. Crawford. He came straight away, but there was nothing he could do. The lilac and laburnum were out, Manningham Lane was lovely with it and I can remember thinking, "It shouldn't be, if Nellie dies she'll never see this". It wasn't right that the trees should look so green, when Nellie wasn't there. It was the custom at that time to keep the corpse at home, and friends would come and peep at her, laid in her coffin, and pay their last respects. They were kind, and this was an expression of their sympathy, and we should have felt hurt if they had not come. The day of the funeral arrived and we were all in black. This was the done thing at this time. Coats were dyed or black ones borrowed (but my parents would never borrow) and somehow we all managed to get complete black. All amusements were banned for three months, so we spent our time going for walks. My auntie came over to stay with us for a while to console us. Life still went on, and time is a great healer; we gradually got round to normal. That summer we went to Bridlington. We were still in mourning, but mother allowed us to wear dresses of mauve or grey, second mourning it was called. Nellie's death made a great impression on me. I should be nearly 18, and life at that time is particularly sweet, but I remember telling my friend that I wished I could die too. I thought it would be much better if all the family could go together. My mother was so sad.

But these thoughts couldn't last, and my mother, as always, turned to work for the cure. We were soon all busy stripping the paper off the bedroom. Then my mother whitewashed the top. Mother was really good at this. She would stand on a table top and always put on an old shirt of my dad's, to take the splashes. When the top was done, all the paint was then washed and polished, every little crack had to be scoured. The lino on the floor was given a good scrub, then the papering could begin. We always got the cheaper papers, so we had to be very careful not to put our fingers through it, when handling it. Mother usually put the paper on. A fire would be lit in the bedroom and all waste bits burnt on it as we went along. There was always someone to do the pasting and wipe the table down after every piece. We were forever standing back and admiring our handiwork, and saying how nice it was going to be when it was done. The papering finished, the carpet would be brought in again and the room put in order. The carpet had first been hung over the clothes line in the yard, and given a good beating. We had a carpet beater which was made of cane, and we took it in turns to give the carpets a good beating, all the dust flying over you. This was only a small carpet, 2 yards by 3 yards, that covered the middle of the floor. After the beating the carpet was given a good shaking by four of us taking a corner each. It was then folded up and taken upstairs. There is something very satisfying about a room that you have cleaned and decorated yourself. The smell of the carbolic lingers. Each time you go in you look round at the decorations, and think how good it is, and congratulate yourself on the fact that there are no creases.

Every year about February time, my mother would get an urge to start spring cleaning. Usually only one room was decorated, the other rooms just had everything taken out or covered whilst the ceiling was swept with a soft brush. Walls were rubbed, paint washed and polished. Then the furniture was polished. Drawers were washed out and put in the sun to dry, or round the fire. Old rubbish was turned out, rugs or carpets given a good cleaning and not until every little nook and cranny had been scoured, was it finished. My father took little part in this. He would put a nail in or turn a screw or do anything else he was asked, but mother didn't think it was a man's job, keeping the house clean was her job along with numerous others, but we all helped and got a lot of fun and satisfaction out of it.

I continued to work at Drummond's in the twisting; our wages had increased and we were now getting about 30/- a week but the cost of living had also increased. There were rumours of the mills going on short time. The queues at the labour exchange got longer as the men came out of the army. Lots of them expecting to get their old job back found the firm closed down or their post filled with someone who would take a lower wage. The men who were boys of 18 when they went away no longer wanted a boy's job, so were compelled to join the ranks of the unemployed; there were always groups of young men on the street corners with nothing to do. We were having trouble over the piece rates in the twisting and I was appointed spokesman to put our case before the manager. I went and knocked on his door; after I while I was admitted, and I put our case. He was an arrogant, bombastic man and when he had finished shouting, I knew that it would be the sack for me; labour was easy to get, and if you didn't like things as they were you could leave. I went back and gave in my notice. My father thought I'd gone mad when I told him, but I'd just had enough of being pushed around. Father was right; he said there would soon be mills on short time with plenty of out-of-works after every job. Well, I left Drummond's and went to sign on.

However, after a few days at home I went to a mill on Canal Road, Unwin Frères, a Belgian firm, in the twisting again. I was given two sides to watch, one of which was just near the crane door. I was on the third floor and had a wonderful view of Bradford. The overlooker here too was a younger man and was much more friendly towards us. But it was here that I had a most frightening experience. It was a lovely summer day and my ends all up, as the phrase is when everything is going smoothly. I had just been looking out of the crane door which was almost always open, when I heard a terrific scream. Looking up, I saw the girl opposite had got her plait fast in the roller of her machine, which of course was still going on. The girl next to her darted forward and stopped the machine. Her plait had gone up the rollers up to her head and every hair was stretched taut and straight. The overlooker came and released her, she sat down for a few minutes and he make her a drink of tea, then advised her to go home; she fixed her hair up, but declined to go home. She sat there while we set her frames on and watched them among us. We all knew why she didn't want to go home; there would have been less money at the weekend. She gradually came round and as the afternoon wore on was able to stand up and do her work, with a little help and a little banter from the rest of us. I think it was in 1921 that Unwins closed down and went back to Belgium. I had been there about two years. We were all given a month's notice; we could leave any time, as we got other employment. This was not so easy, as several mills had closed down and others were on short time. I stayed till the last week. Unwins doubled our last week's wage; we were stunned when we heard this, such wealth had not come our way before. I drew over £5.

Chapter 9

Out of the Mill

Scanning the paper for any chance of a job, I saw an advert for a young lady at Singers sewing machine shop, and the more I thought about it the more I liked it, and decided I would go and apply. At last my dad asked me if I had found anything. I said, "Yes, they want someone at Singers". He said, "Yes and they'll offer you about ten shillings a week". I said, "Well they won't get me then". The following morning I went and applied; I was told they wanted someone to follow up on their sales by going to the homes of customers and showing them how to use the attachments for tucking, binding, gathering etc., that were with every machine. The wage was twenty-five shillings a week and my expenses paid. I took the job, because the mills were slack and I thought at least I could pay my jock brass and I had no wish to go and join the queues at the labour exchange. At this time I was paying eighteen shillings a week at home, so I was left with seven shillings for clothes and spending money. I had saved a little and felt I could manage.

I enjoyed this work. I was out of the mill. I had a training period of about two weeks; the manageress at the Manningham Lane shop taught me the use of all the attachments. I worked from nine to six-thirty with an hour off for dinner. Oh the joy of not having to get up at six o'clock in the morning. I think Singers were the pioneers in this country for selling by weekly instalments. The salesmen, about eight or ten, came to the shop each morning and reported any sales. I was then given the addresses and went along to show the lady of the house how to use the machine. I had quite an eye-opener at some of the houses I went to. I had always been brought up in a working-class district with never anything to spare, but our houses were always clean, the steps outside washed and scoured every week with a yellow or white line decorating the edge of each step; yards were swept and periodically swilled, rubbish was not allowed to accumulate—it was either burnt or smashed up and put in the midden. Now I was sent to some of the most abject slums. The salesmen unable to make a sale that week, would talk some of these people into having a machine just on trial. He would get his commission, which would be forfeited later if the payments were not made, but at least it had tided him over for a few more days. It surprised me to learn how many people could be talked into having a machine which they did not really want, and would pay a few instalments, then let it go back when they found they needed the money for something else. I remarked on this to one lady, when she told me the machine was going back. I said, "Yes, but you've lost three weeks' instalments". She smiled and said, "Not really love, you see I take sewing in and I waited till I had several jobs. I've been working night and day these last few weeks and I've made quite a bit. Now I've worked myself up, but if I get some more jobs in a month or two I can always get another machine on trial". It was quite true and I had to admire her for her ingenuity.

I usually planned my work each morning, and I had cards to be signed at each house I visited, just to prove I had been there. I would have the visits approved by the manager who generally added another one or two, saying, "Oh, you're going to Heaton; well, just call in here at Daisy Hill"—a mile away—"it won't take you long". I was then given my tram-fares, I don't think it was ever more than 8d. in one day, and off I went. At first I remember going to the shop each evening, but this was discontinued, and I took enough work out with me to last the day. It was very rare that I arrived home before six-thirty, as I always had at least one customer who did not get home from work till after six. I was conscientious and I enjoyed my work. I liked the teaching part, and must have taught dozens of people to use the attachments, but I don't know anyone who really used them (except myself). However I suppose it all helped the sales. I liked meeting people; I found them pleasant and always ready to make me a cup of tea.

I remember having calls to make at Thornton one afternoon, two of them after five o'clock. I had a drink of tea during the afternoon at one of the ladies', who when she brought it in produced a boiled egg and bread and butter, saying she was a little peckish herself. Well I enjoyed that, but at the next house the lady was just making tea and boiling eggs. "You'll have one won't you? You young lasses are always hungry, I know because I have some". It was no use me talking; I had another egg, then quite a walk to the next house. I hadn't to be there till after six, but when I was again offered a cup of tea and a boiled egg and the man of the house capped it by saying, "Put her two in, she's a long way to go before she gets home", well, I just gave in. It was no use saying I had already had tea and wasn't hungry; they just insisted, and somehow I got through the eggs.

Sometimes the menfolk were quite interested in the machine and learned to thread it up and treadle, and I was always pleased to show them as I thought it was much better if two people knew how to manage it. Once when I was demonstrating the use of the needle threader, a little contraption consisting of a piece of metal with a tiny hook like a crochet hook which slipped into the eye of the needle—you then brought your cotton over the hook and drew it through the eye; it was very simple when you got the knack of it—well, the man of the house had been watching, while his wife made a few futile attempts; then he had a go and managed it the first attempt, saying all the time, "Tha mon ger it anent eye, tha mon ger it anent eye".

I walked miles going from one place to another; the Bradford district covered a large area, although I did not go as far as the buses of today do. I would go to the places not so far out in the mornings—though the visits had to be fitted in to the customers' convenience too—then after dinner I went further afield. I loved going up to Queensbury. The old trams took about half an hour; if it was a nice day I would sit upstairs and enjoy the view. There was a space at the top that was open to the weather, only having a roof. You could sit in this elevated position and feel the wind, the rain, or the sun on your face as the case might be. I got to really know Bradford. At that time the trams only went as far as Baildon Bridge, so if I had any calls at Baildon it meant walking from that point. The Allerton trams went as far as the top of Allerton, so you walked to Wilsden. It was a long way, but how I enjoyed those walks. All weathers I went out and loved to feel the rain on my face. While standing on the hills round Bradford I would try to imagine what it had been like a hundred years ago, before all those great mills had sprung up. I would look at those great chimneys belching forth their black smoke, and thank God that I had at last got out of the mill and was able to support myself. I began to see and love the Yorkshire dales, as sometimes I was sent to Steeton, Silsden, Haworth, Keighley and Skipton, where I worked for a few months. While there I went to lots of the little villages round about. I remember going to Giggleswick College one lovely day, and being shown round part of it by the housekeeper. I also went to Bolton Hall, again being shown round by the housekeeper.

Life was good, and I knew now that whatever happened, I should not go back into the mill; that part was finished. I had had a rise in wages after being at Singer's for a month. I was also asked to take cottons to sell to the customers on commission; this usually brought in another two shillings a week, so my wage was almost thirty shillings a week. The mills at this time were suffering a depression and wages had dropped, so if I had returned I should not have got a bigger wage than I was now receiving. I continued to tramp my way around, content to put up with the dirty and disagreeable side of the work in order to enjoy the pleasanter part.

Soon after I started at Singers the manageress in the shop left and was replaced by a girl, Eva Beecroft, who became a great friend of mine and we went about quite a lot together. I had kept up my swimming so we generally managed to go to the baths once a week. Sometimes my sisters would join us. Drummond Road baths was our venue, and we spent some happy times there. The bath attendant at that time was a Mr. Call, and he was very helpful and improved our stroke. My eldest sister I had taught to swim, for which she bought me a new costume. I thought it was a smasher, it was navy blue stockinette with a band of pale blue around the neck and across the legs. The arms came down to the elbows and the legs halfway down the thighs. Bella, who was working in the weaving at this time and was a bit better off than me joined the club at the Windsor baths and went in for the R.L.S.S. Bronze Medallion. She then wanted to go a bit further and take the R.L.S.S. Instructor's Certificate, so she roped Eva and me into a class of six girls. She trained us and we both passed the exam and got our Bronze Medal. We never went in for any competitive swimming. During the war there hadn't been any chance, and now we were too old for racing. We would occasionally go to the open air pool in Lister Park as it was called; it was later called the Lido.

Eva Beecroft was keen on walking, and we would plan walks for the weekend. Their family, four boys and one girl, were all keen workers for the labour movement. Harry, the elder, often spoke at Labour meetings. Mrs. Beecroft was a fine woman I much admired, she could talk for hours about the politicians of the day, and was an untiring worker for the Labour cause. At that time a lot of young people would go to the Clarion Club House on Otley Chevin where you could get a cup of tea, and if the weather was fine, walk along the top, admiring the wonderful view. Discussions would be held out in the open, just sitting on the grass eating our sandwiches. We spent many happy Saturday afternoons there. Eva was much more concerned about the problems of the day than I had been, but I soon came round to her way of thinking, and was quite willing to help all I could to get a better deal for the workers. We were both members of the Guild of Youth—I should think that this was the first youth club—and while working for the cause we managed to arrange some very pleasant outings. We had rambles over Ilkley Moors and Bolton Abbey, shorter ones on Sunday evenings when we would go round Cottingley and Bingley or up onto Shipley Glen. We approached the Education Committee to give us land for a tennis court, and finally, after a lot of worrying, we were told we could have a piece of land at

Fairweather Green. Well, it was on a slope, it was all bumps and hollows, it was all overgrown with weeds and all the Corporation would do was cut down the weeds. We then went and started digging. The young men really worked hard and we helped. We tried to level it, then roll it, and all this was done in the evenings. We walked across one or two nights a week, worked hard for an hour, then it would be time to start walking home again. We just tumbled into bed and fell fast asleep after that. At last it was flattened. The Corporation came and marked it out for us, and we started teaching each other how to play tennis. Rackets and balls were scarce, but we managed, and had great fun. It was ours, and every night there would be about a dozen of us sat about talking while we waited for a game. We followed the book of instruction, and learned the rudiments of the game. Later on we dared to go to the public courts in the park and enjoyed lots of games there.

Most of the young people in the Guild were very serious thinkers and were determined to get a better deal for the workers of this country, so a lot of our time was taken up with work for the Labour Party. It was about this time too that the Labour Party took St George's Hall for their speakers every Saturday night and I had the pleasure of hearing some of the finest politicians of the day speak in that hall to capacity crowds. After the meeting we would sell the labour paper to the crowds as they left. My father would argue with me sometimes about the Labour Party. He remained a staunch Conservative. Don't you see, he would say, the Conservatives are educated and you must have educated men at the top. To which I would reply, and what's wrong with the Labour people being educated? We know we are ignorant and if a university education is good for the monied class, then it is good for the worker and that's just what we want: the chance to go on, and go to the University and learn to express ourselves, so that we can have a voice in the government. Now the principles of the Labour movement had been studied and accepted by men of integrity, men who cared, and it was beginning to make itself felt as a vital force. In 1924 we had our first Labour Government, under the leadership of Mr. Ramsay MacDonald. They continued to hold office until November when Mr. Stanley Baldwin's Cabinet was announced.

We went to the theatre occasionally and I remember climbing up into the Gods at the Old Empire to hear Florrie Forde. What a wonderful trouper she was. She captivated the audience right from the start. She was so full of life and put such a lot of feeling into her singing. I shall never forget her singing "Oh, Oh Antonio", "Where are the lads of the village tonight", "Row me on the river Romeo", "How're you going to keep them down on the farm" and, oh, a host of others. I saw Bransby

Williams on the stage at the old Prince's Theatre. He was great in his portrayal of Dickens characters and had us all weeping at Little Nell's Grandfather. These were great times on the stage with great actors and actresses.
Now we watch them on the television and it is nice and cosy, but we miss
the atmosphere and all the excitement that went with a trip to the theatre.
Mcanwhile on the films Rudolf Valentino was capturing the audiences.
There were great queues wherever he was appearing and women swooned
at the sight of him, much as the young people of today do, at the sight of
their favourite pop groups. Lawn tennis was becoming much more popular and the Wimbledon games were followed and discussed by the
workers. Madam Lenglen was our heroine and we all wore headbands
that she made so popular.

I remember 1924 because it was in this year that I made my first visit to
London. My sister Bella and I decided that we would visit the Wembley
Exhibition. This had taken some saving up for. We were fortunate that
Bella had some friends she had made while in service, two sisters who
had a flat, and as one of them was out on a job they lent us the use of
it. The other sister was at home, more or less retired. She was an enor-
mous woman, who spent most of her time in bed reading magazines. I
never saw any evidence of cooking; she seemed to subsist on cups of tea
and biscuits. However she was very kind and let us have the run of the flat.

We came up to London on a four day trip. One day was spent travelling.
We boarded the train at 9.30 a.m. and arrived at King's Cross at 6.30. It
was quite an experience. Bella had been in London several times and knew
her way around, but it was all very new and exciting to me. We went by
underground to St John's Wood where we were staying and after having
a meal we went for a short walk and then to bed. The following morning
we were up early and made our way to Wembley. It was a glorious hot day
and there was so much to see. There was a model railway which you could
ride on, but we contented ourselves with watching this. There was a model
of the Taj Mahal, which was really beautiful. There was also a model of
the Gold Coast which looked absolutely wonderful. We made our way
round to the amusements and went on the big dipper, which I thought
was terrifying, and I've never been on one since. What a day that was!
The following day we spent sightseeing, going to Buckingham Palace
and Hyde Park. Then the next day we came home. We had quite a lot
to talk about for a long time; there weren't many of our acquaintances
who had been to London.

Well the unemployment problem got steadily worse, mills were on short
time, the miners were asked to take a reduction in wages and refused, and
altogether things were looking pretty grim. The General Council of the

Trade Unions called a National Strike and industrial workers throughout the country ceased work. It seemed very queer; such a lot could be written about these times. Eventually some of the services were manned by a volunteer brigade, mostly young students.

Meanwhile I was still going on my rounds. The mills were all closed and very little work was going on. The weather was glorious. Early Spring with lilac and laburnum just ready for flowering. I remember being up on the hills at Daisy Hill on a lovely clear day. Bradford lay down in the valley, all those mill chimneys and no smoke belching from them, miles and miles could I see and it was lovely. I thought what a lovely place this would be if only we could do without the smoke. I have lived to see the smokeless zone, and it is almost as bonny a picture as I saw that day. It is just spoiled perhaps by the huge blocks of flats that have sprung up in the meantime, but at least the air is cleaner. I like to think we have made at least some progress, from the ugly and depressing past.

I was soon to get a shock and my little world turned upside down again. The manager called me into the office one morning and gave me a week's notice. He had received notice from headquarters that owing to reduction in sales, they were going to discontinue the teaching service, and in future the salesmen would follow their own sales, by teaching the customer how to use the machine, and the customer could go to the shop for any further instruction on the attachments. The shop manageress would teach them; I was therefore redundant. The manager was very sorry, but there was nothing he could do about it. This was a great blow to me. I was very happy in this work, and could not think of any other work I could do that would take me outside like this had done. However there was nothing to do except go home with the news.

At home things were not too bad. Lizzie and Annie were both married and had got homes of their own. Lizzie's husband was a fireman. He had joined the fire service after coming out of the army. Annie's husband was in the police force; he too had joined after coming out of the army. George had come home and was now out of work. He had no trade, and had worked in the mill, but now the mills were all on slack time and jobs were hard to find and didn't last long when found. Charlie had come home and gone back to the railway. Alice was still working in the mill; she was courting and hoping to get married later that year. Jim was working; he had been apprenticed to a joiner and had almost finished his apprenticeship. Hetty was still working in the mill. Lillian was working in a shop in town, and Harry was with a catering firm. As a family we could manage; individually we had very little.

Well, the end of the week came, and I went down to the Labour

Exchange the following Monday morning. How I hated going, but I had no choice. The mills were not taking any new workers and for every job advertised there were dozens of applicants. I had quite a long wait in the queue, and when it was my turn I was asked my last job, dates of starting and finishing, what I did before that, and that, and that, going right back to when I started full time at the age of fourteen. They had nothing to offer me, and I was told to come again and sign on the Wednesday and again on the Friday. At that time the dole was 15s. a week, so I hadn't my jock brass as I was paying 18s. a week at home. I took the money home and my mother gave me 2s. 6d. back, and we went on like this while I was out of work. This was the first time in eleven years that I had been out of work, and I did not like it. I answered all kinds of advertisements but I seemed to be really up against it and the weeks slipped by. I was able to help in the house, and I altered dresses and made old ones into new ones or into aprons. We were always making do and mending. I had a friend who had a navy blue serge costume so long that it faded and was going a lovely shade of red and purple. She couldn't afford a new one, so she unpicked every stitch, pressed the pieces out and turned them. The inside was not faded at all, and it looked lovely and was worn a few more years. I didn't go as far as that, but I did do a lot of sewing, and helping to decorate the house. Twice a week I went down to the Labour Exchange, but when I asked about any work, there was nothing. This went on for two months and I was really thinking I should have to go into service.

Chapter 10

Probationer Nurse

Then one night, when I was scanning the jobs vacant column, I said to my mother "What about this?", and I read out to her:

Probationer nurses wanted, Menston Asylum. No previous experience necessary. Wages £2 2s. per week, from which 19s. will be deducted for food.

That would leave me with 23s. per week. My mother said, "Well try if you like, but you'll never stick it". The next morning I was up early and went to Menston. It was a lovely day, and as I walked down the long drive to the hospital I saw several groups of male patients with their nurses, working in the gardens. Feeling very nervous, I kept on, and rang the bell at the porter's lodge. The porter came and I told him I had come in answer to the advertisement. He said, "Oh yes. Well I shall just have to fill this form in before I take you to see matron". He then asked my name and age. He also weighed me and took my height. He said I was about half an inch too small, but he would forget it. He put the required height down. He then took me to the matron's office, announced me, and left. I was left standing in front of the matron's desk. She was busy with some papers and ignored me for a time; she then looked up, and invited me to sit down, and turned to the form the porter had left on her desk. She asked me where I had worked before, and why I had chosen to seek employment there. I answered truthfully that I wanted work and that I had been unable to get any. She asked me about my home and religion, and told me the work there would be very hard. All the time she was filling the form up with my answers. Then she got up and thanked me for coming, and said I would receive word in a few days as to whether I had been accepted, and that was the end of the interview. I liked the matron. I felt that she could be very nice, but she looked very tired to me; she must have been near sixty. I walked down the drive wondering what kind of impression I had made and feeling a bit apprehensive about the job. I went home and related to the family all that had happened, and the general verdict was that I would not be accepted.

"Probationer nurses wanted, Menston Asylum"
High Royds Hospital, Menston.
Drawing by J.O. Chapman, 1988. (Courtesy High Royds Hospital)

Well there was nothing to do but wait and see. About ten days later I received an official form saying I had been accepted and would I report for duty the following Monday at 1 p.m. I was really pleased, though I still felt a little apprehensive. This was something altogether different. I was leaving home again. I should have one full day a week off; any other time I should have to apply for a pass out. I think I was a little afraid. Then I thought, but you are not going back to the mill. Hurrah, anything is better than that! I had prayed about getting a job, and wondered if this was the answer. I told my Sunday School teacher, Miss Ackroyd, but she rather thought I ought to have stayed at home. However, by the following Monday I was quite happy to go, and with the thought that I am really out of the mill, I've been out four years and I'm not going back, I went up the drive again and rang the bell.

The porter came and I told him who I was. "Oh", he said, "you'll have to see the matron". He took me along a wide corridor. He had a bunch of keys, and at the end of the corridor he unlocked the door, carefully locked it again, and went on. This happened three times before we came to the matron's office. He knocked on the door, opened it, announced me, and, closing the door after me, retired. The matron told me I should be expected to start my duties the following morning. For the first two or three weeks I should be on office hours, nine to five-thirty, with one hour off for dinner. "You will be given a list of rules which you are expected to obey. You will have one day off a week. You are expected to report for duty clean, tidy, and properly dressed. I don't like to see my nurses without cuffs or caps. You must at all times when on the ward wear black stockings and flat-heeled shoes. I will show you to your room. I have had a fire lit, because the day is cold and the room has not been used for some time. The night nurse sleeps opposite you, so you will be as quiet as possible during the day. Fires are not allowed in your room, so tomorrow you will clean the grate out, and at all times you must keep your room clean and tidy. Cleaning requisites will be found in the bathroom at the end of the corridor". We had now reached my room, where a miserable fire burned in the grate. She turned to go, saying she would have my uniform sent up to me. "Oh, and there will be a bunch of keys—your own door key, and a master key for all the doors on the corridors and wards— and just guard those keys, they must not get into the wrong hands". I thanked her and promised to take care of the keys. She said, "Now you had better unpack, then go down to Ward 16, where you will be tomorrow and where you will get your tea. Your rations will be sent there".

She left me. I looked round the room. There was a bed which I tested and thought would be fine. A wardrobe and a dressing table. On the floor was a nice strip of red carpet spoiled with the words "Menston Asylum" written over it. However, I thought on the whole it could be very nice when I got a cover on the table and a few pieces. There was a chair by the side of the bed, on which I put my alarm clock and my bible. Then I looked round for a poker. There wasn't one, but I found a chip of wood and stirred the fire up. Then I remembered about the night nurse and thought I'd better keep quiet. A maid came up with my uniform, which she dumped on the bed, saying, "This room is cold. You want to put some bottles in this bed". We chatted a few minutes. Then she said, "Well, I must be off". I looked at the uniform. There were two grey dresses. I tried them on. They were a tight fit but quite allright. They came down almost to my ankles. There were three aprons, three caps, three collars, and three pairs of cuffs. I put one of the dresses in front of the fire to air, and I put the other things I should want the following morning on the chair. I unpacked my case, and then I felt it was teatime, but I didn't know where to go, and there didn't seem to be anyone to ask. "Well", I thought, "You had better go and find out", so taking my bunch of keys I crept quietly out.

I went down the steps at the end of the corridor without meeting any-one, so I continued along another corridor, unlocking the door and lock-ing it carefully after me. Here I met a nurse who directed me to Ward 16, where I found the kitchen and went in. I sat down and looked around. After a while a nurse came in, said "hello" to me, and went straight out again. I still sat there. There was a coal fire and it felt warm and comfor-table. The nurse came back again and sat down. She said, "You'll be the new probationer". I said, "Yes". She said, "Well, I'm just going to have my tea so you can join me. They've sent some liver up, so if you like to be cooking it, I'll cut some bread". She spoke with a strong Irish brogue, and seemed very friendly. Just then she was called on to the ward. I put a piece of butter in the frying pan and put it on the gas stove. I put some liver in, cut some bread, found the crockery and cutlery, and set the table. The kettle was boiling so I brewed the tea. I saw a 7 lb. jar of jam, so I put some on a saucer. The nurse came in again, looked at the table, and said, "That's fine". I dished the liver out and poured the tea. I was ready for mine, having had an early dinner. The nurse turned to me and said, "My name's Norah". I said, "Mine's Maggie". She said, "We are not allowed to use Christian names, so it's Sister Malony and Nurse Lount". Another nurse, Hilda, to be called Nurse Thompson, came in for her tea, and Sister Malony went on the ward. After tea I cleared away and was starting to wash up when Nurse Thompson said, "Leave that. One of the patients comes in to do it, and she would be upset if anyone else did it".

I then saw my week's rations on a side table. There was about a pound of sugar, half a pound of butter, and a quarter of tea. There was also a small loaf; this we got each day. I asked what I did with them, and was advised to take them up to my room and bring them down as required, otherwise they would be scrounged. I took the tea and butter but left the sugar; as I didn't take sugar I was not greatly worried if it was scrounged. The bread I took with me, thinking I might have some for sup-per. We had had nothing but margarine for years, so bread and butter would be a real treat. I learned later that we were not supposed to eat in our own rooms.

The sister and the nurses were busy on the ward now, so I went to my room. There didn't seem to be anything to do until bedtime. I filled my hot water bottle at the bathroom and put it in the bed. Then I drew a chair up to the fire and looked at a magazine I had brought with me. It was now about 6 p.m. and wet and cold outside. I wondered if I should wake up in time in the morning; it would be awful if I was late. Although there were many rooms on this floor I had not heard or seen anyone. I set my alarm clock and sat down again with the magazine. At about 9 p.m. the fire was almost out and there was no more coal. I had a couple of slices of bread and butter and went to bed.

The following morning I woke about 7 a.m. It was dark. I lay a few minutes, then got up. I made no noise as I went down to the bathroom. After dressing I tidied my room, leaving the grate to clear out later. Then I collected my butter and tea and went down for breakfast. Everything was in a bustle in the kitchen. However, I saw a jar of marmalade, so I made my breakfast of marmalade and bread. There were two patients busy washing up, and I talked to them a while. Then as it neared 9 a.m. I thought I had better report to the Sister. She was on the ward. She said, "You'd better help me with these beds. Nurse Jones is away and I am here by myself". There would be between thirty and forty beds in the ward, which was almost square, so that there were two lines of beds down the middle as well as one at each side. We started going round, getting each patient out for the toilet or giving them the bed pan, making the bed, and getting them back in. We had no time for talking, but I noticed that the sister had a word for most of the patients. This was the sick ward, and some were very ill apart from their mental disorder. The beds were finished at about 10.30. Then the sister went into the kitchen, raked some hot cinders onto a shovel, picked up a bottle of disinfectant, and went back on the ward. Then occasionally pouring a few drops of disinfectant on the hot cinders, she walked up and down the aisles holding the shovel high, purifying the air. This job was just completed when in came the doctor on his morning round. The sister of course followed him a step behind. I went and did some dusting.

When the doctor left I was told to go to the day room and keep the patients quiet there. This was a huge drawing room, with a fireplace and a lovely fire behind a strong fireguard with a lock on. I found a key for this on my bunch of keys. There was silence as I went in. The ladies were walking about or sitting in the comfortable chairs round the fire. I was new, and they were wondering what I was like. I said, "Good morning ladies. I hope you are all warm and comfortable. I see it's raining heavy outside, and it's very cold". There was more silence. Then one or two of them said good morning and went on with their conversations. I went over to the large bow window and looked out. I saw a well-kept lawn, surrounded by a wide path and flowering shrubs. Everything was heavy with rain and looked rather depressing. Some of the patients came and joined me, and I talked to them, but often they changed the subject abruptly, and sometimes they got near quarrelling with each other. Then I was peacemaker; I didn't want any quarrels on my first day. They asked where I came from. I told them, and those who knew Bradford were keen to hear about it, and started talking of days gone by. One lady asked me for my keys, as she wanted to go home. Another said, "Don't give her them, nurse, she's always trying it on, and she'll get you into trouble". I had no intention of giving her the keys, but I talked to her and said we would all go together soon, and she seemed satisfied. The sister looked in and told two of the patients to go with me for coal. We filled six buckets. The two patients were both young, not much older than myself, and at times were quite sane, but at other times if upset would go off into a paddy and curse everything and everybody. There were three padded cells where patients were put if they became too violent, in order to protect themselves as much as others. When they became violent they seemed to possess extra strength, and it often took two and sometimes three of us to deal with them. We didn't have any violence this morning, but we were kept busy all the time; the wards were all understaffed.

We had a cup of tea at 11.30. Dinners were served at 12.00. I helped the sister to serve the bed patients. Then she told me to take the day room patients to the dining room, saying, "They will show you the way. You serve them and bring them back". We went to a large dining hall, where there were other nurses with patients from other wards. I soon saw what was expected. The nurses queued with plates, and a sister served the dinners, until all the patients were served. I began to feel a bit hungry, but I knew I should have to wait for my dinner. The nurses worked on shifts, 6 a.m. to 12 p.m., 2 p.m. to 10; dinner was served between 1 p.m. and 2. The night shift was 10 p.m. to 6 a.m. Dinner was in the nurses' dining hall. We sat at a long table; at the head of it the sister would carve the meat and pass it along, or serve the chops, mince, or whatever. Tureens of vegetables followed. Grace was said, and we started. On the whole the food was good and enjoyable, though we had our fair share of bread-and-butter puddings and jam roly-poly.

After dinner I went back to my room, had a wash and brush up, and went straight back to the ward. The afternoon was very much like the morning. There was an extra nurse in the ward, so I stayed in the day room, trying to keep the patients happy. At about 4.30 we started with the teas, but I went off duty at 5.00, so I went to the kitchen and made myself some tea. We had our rations and there was always the 7 lb. jar of plum and apple jam. We could make toast. Something was always sent up for us when they sent the patients' teas. We were sent kippers, liver, eggs, currant pasty, or spice loaf, but most often kippers. Which was rather a pity, as there never seemed time or anyone to cook them.

But there was always the jam; why always plum and apple I don't know, but now when I see plum and apple jam I think of the kitchens at Menston.

When I had finished tea I went up to my room and lay on my bed for a while. I didn't dare light the fire, though it felt cold after the warm wards. I cleaned the grate, dusted round, and had a bath. As there didn't seem to be anything else to do I went to bed early. The next day a nurse asked me what I had done the previous evening, and when I told her she said, "Oh, you should have gone down to the nurses' room. There is generally someone there, and there are books and magazines". This sounded quite good, and I decided to go down that night, if only to relax in front of the fire in a comfortable chair.

I spent the first week on Ward 16. One morning I went into a side room for some cleaning equipment, and was startled to see a nurse sewing calico covering round the body of a patient. She looked up and said, "It's allright, she's dead. This should be your job, but as you are new I said I would do it". I thanked her and hurried out, hoping no one else died while I was on duty. This morning was fine, so at about 10.30 the nurse said, "Slip a coat or cardigan on, we are going to take the patients out for exercise". The day patients put cardigans on, and we all went out into the garden. We got the patients more or less in twos in crocodile, and with the nurse at the front and me at the rear we walked round and round the square. It felt good to be out, and some of the patients were quite interested in the flowers and shrubs that looked so fresh after the rain. We stayed out for an hour.

The following week I was on Ward 15. It was a sick ward too, and the routine was much the same. My training was then completed, and I went onto normal shift work. On the Sunday before that it was my day off, so I went home. I went for a walk in the afternoon and was tired when I got back to Menston, so I went to bed early. I was scared to death I should not wake up in time to go on the ward at 6 a.m. I did not sleep for some time, and kept waking up. At about 5.00 I decided to get up in case I fell off to sleep again. I had no idea what went on in the ward before 9 a.m. The sister on duty told me to get the day room patients up, get them washed, and take them in to breakfast at 7.00. I had to find some matches to light the gas lamps on the stairs and in the dormitory. I then called the patients to get up. Some were up in a flash, but others were awkward, and it is not easy trying to get twenty women washed and their hair combed in about forty minutes. There were only two wash basins. However we were in good time for breakfast, which consisted of porridge, followed by bread and jam. Afterwards the patients were taken to the day room, and I did various jobs till the sister sent me for my breakfast. I had fried bacon. The bacon at Menston was always thick and chunky, but it made nice dip for your bread, and I enjoyed it.

We were now beginning to think about Christmas. Whenever we could find the time, we would get crinkly coloured paper and scissors, and start making flowers. The patients helped in making these, and the making of them certainly helped the patients. We thought that if the patients had something to do it was better for them, but supervision was always a problem. Usually there was only a sister and a nurse on duty at one time, to a ward of forty patients or more. We encouraged them to do whatever they were able. We had a piano, and those patients who could play were allowed to use it, so now we tried to make time to practise Christmas carols. We decorated the ward with our paper flowers. We had made roses, and I thought I had never seen finer decorations. The week before Christmas we took some of the patients round the other wards to see the other decorations. One ward was easily the best; they had made orchids in all shades of purple. Christmas week was given over to festivities as much as possible. I was fortunate that my day off came on Christmas day, so I was able to go home.

I had settled down to the life at Menston and was quite happy. I went home on my days off, and my mother would usually send me back with a few home-made teacakes, or an apple pie. She was sure we didn't get enough to eat, though I assured her that we did. Whenever I called to see my friend Eva Beecroft her mother would send me back with a large oven cake, and didn't we enjoy them for supper! I now knew quite a few of the nurses, as I was sent to other wards, and also met them in the nurses' room, where we had sing-songs round the piano. We had a religious service in the chapel every Sunday morning, which was always well attended. We also had a dance every Friday evening, which nurses were encouraged to attend even if not on duty. We were not allowed to dance with each other, or with the male nurses who brought the men, but only with the patients, some of whom were very good dancers.

After Christmas I was put on night duty for a week, and met the night sister who roomed opposite me. I had been careful always to appear on the ward properly dressed in cuffs, collar, and cap, although sometimes if we thought there was no fear of Matron coming round we would loosen our collars and remove our cuffs. On my first night I saw Matron arrive, and the night sister came over to me and whispered, "Give me your cuffs". She slipped them on before meeting the Matron. I carried on with my sleeves rolled back. Night duty was very tiring. Some of the patients were fretful and couldn't sleep. The sister told me to make some tea, and she gave this to some of them. It surprised me how gentle and kind she was with the patients, because she was very abrupt with the nurses, and not at all friendly. The morning came at last and I made a meal in the kitchen; then we went off duty and to bed. I got up about 4 p.m., went out for an hour, had tea, and went to the recreation room to read until it was time to go down to dinner before going on duty at 10.

The following week I went on day duty again, but this time in a different ward. The patients were noisier and more aggressive. There were about eighty of them; there was a sister, another nurse, and myself. Some of the patients helped with polishing the floor, fetching the coal, and various other little jobs. Bathing day was quite a business. We started at about 9.30 and had to have finished at 11.50. We had two baths. We kept letting a little water out and adding a little fresh. No time was wasted; it was in the bath, a good soaping and rubbing, hair washed and a jug of water poured over to rinse it, then out and a rub. They were left to finish drying themselves and get dressed. I was really tired after my first morning on the bathing parade.

The following week I did two nights on the epileptic ward, another big one, with sixty patients. We were short of staff, because there were several nurses down with flu. My first night on this ward was a bit grim. The sister who should have been with me had been working all the day. She told me my duties and stayed with me till about 11 p.m. Then she went off to try and get some rest; there was a push button bell connected with her room, which I was told to use if I needed any help. All the patients seemed very quiet, and I just hoped everything would be all right and I would be able to manage. The lights were turned out and I sat at a table at the end of the ward. With the light from my lamp I was able to look at a magazine. I had been told to make my rounds of the beds every hour or oftener if I thought anyone needed assistance. I had just finished my first round when I heard a thud. One of the patients had gone into a fit and fallen out of bed. Another patient immediately came to my aid, and said, "Leave her nurse, she'll be all right, and there's somebody over there just gone off". I went over to this patient, who was biting badly, and gave her something to bite on. My assistant reported that the first patient was allright. I went back to her and got her to bed. Now there was a third. There isn't much you can do for an epileptic except see that they don't hurt themselves. After a while we got them all settled, and my assistant said, "Shall I go and make a cup of tea?" I said, "Yes", and then wondered if I should have allowed her into the kitchen; however, she was soon back with a tray with tea

Maggie (centre) and colleagues at Menston Hospital. February 1926
(Photo courtesy of James Ogden)

and biscuits. We took a cup to each of the patients who had been ill, and then sat down to ours; she took the cups away and washed up before she went back to bed. At about four o'clock two more patients went off. My assistant was asleep, but I watched them, and gradually they came round. I made them a drink of tea, had one myself, and sat down to wait till 6 a.m. for the day nurse. I reported to the sister about the patients who had been ill and about my helper. She said, "Yes, she is good, and could go home, if she had one, but she has no one". The second night on the epileptic ward, which I rather dreaded, passed off without incident.

I was then put back on day duty on the sick ward. We were into February now. It was very cold, and we had quite a lot of snow. Getting the coal in was quite a job, as it was stacked in the yard and covered with snow. We usually had plenty of volunteers, but we had to be careful whom we took, as some of them might get a little playful and start throwing lumps of coal about. Once we had just filled our buckets when one of the patients emptied them all. I had to talk to her while the others filled them again; I dare not leave them while I took her in, or there would probably have been more trouble. Besides, it was a rule never to leave a patient for a minute outside, although we were in a walled yard with locked doors.

One day I was taking my rations up to my room when I met Grace, a nurse whom I had made a friend of. We stopped for a chat. She said, "Where's your sugar?" I said I'd left it on the ward. She asked if she could have it and I said yes. She said, "What about your loaf?" I said, "Take it, I've plenty of yesterday's, but why, what about your own rations?" She told me she was going home to Newcastle for the week-end. She said, "I've packed all my rations and I've saved a large tin of tea which I'm taking". I was amazed and asked, "Is it right to do so?" She answered, "They are my rations, and right or wrong I'm taking them. My father's out of work and there's seven of them at home. My sister started work after Christmas but there are four younger than her". I said, "Here, you had better take my tea, I can manage". It brought home to me how much unemployment there was, and I was thankful I had got work that I liked, and could keep myself. I told my parents next time I got home. My father immediately said, "Don't you start bringing anything home. We can manage, and it's not right—that food is given to you for your use'. I said, "Yes, but if there is too much, the bread only goes to the pigs". But he was adamant, and I never took any food home.

I had no intention of leaving Menston, but had to do, through illness. About a week later the snow had gone, it was a fine morning, and we took the patients out for exercise. I had not felt well when I went on duty at 6 a.m., and by the time we had finished the exercise I felt decidedly sick and cold. I was just taking my coat off when I heard a voice far away saying, "Look out, nurse". I had fainted. When I came round I was put to bed and the doctor was sent for. It was influenza. I had a high temperature for a few days, and had to stay in bed for over a week, when I was allowed to get up for a few hours. By the end of the second week I was up for a whole day, and was told Matron wanted to see me. I went along to her room. She asked me to sit down, and said, "You have been very ill and you still need rest. Therefore we are sending you home. Your heart is weak and you must see your own doctor, but the great thing is rest and fresh air". I asked if I could have a month's leave and then return. She said she was sorry, but she was afraid I should never be strong enough for the work there. If I felt like it, after a year's absence I might apply again. She was sorry to lose me and advised me to get an outdoor job for a while. This was indeed a blow. I was quite happy at Menston, had put my name down for a series of lectures, and had intended to try and get on in this work. I went to my room and started to pack. Grace came to see me and I told her the news. She said, "Oh what rotten luck! Never mind, perhaps when you are a little stronger you will be able to get in at one of the children's hospitals. The work is not so heavy there. I'm going to try myself next year". She helped me with my packing, and I went down and said my goodbyes. Then Grace went with me to the bus stop, and I went home.

Chapter 11

Swimming Teacher

When I arrived home my mother took one look at me and said, "It's bed for you". Indeed I was glad to go. I had lost nearly a stone in weight and felt decidedly tired. The doctor came the following day, and told me to stay in bed till he came the next day. The weather was wet and cold, and I was glad to stay where I was, warm and comfortable, and be looked after. However, in about a fortnight I was much better, and beginning to think about work again. The doctor advised light outdoor work, as my heart was still weak.

I had no idea what I could do, but kept looking at the advertisements in the paper till I saw one that looked interesting. 'A young lady wanted as waitress, at Masham Café, Manningham Park: season only, April to September.' It was now the middle of March. I went along the following morning, got the job, and started the following week. My hours were 10 a.m. till 7 or sometimes 8 p.m. I was paid eighteen shillings a week and got my dinner and tea on the job. There were two of us besides the proprietor, Mr Dixon, and his daughter. Mr Dixon did all the odd jobs and made the icecream, which was renowned. His daughter served at the counter and looked after the till. The busiest times were in the afternoons, especially on hot days. We served snacks, but pots of tea and sandwiches were our biggest line, and we sold hundreds of them. I soon adapted myself to this work. I usually walked home in the evening and it was soon bedtime, but I didn't have to get up early and I began to feel much better. I enjoyed the walk through the park in the morning. The long summer days were made to be enjoyed, and we enjoyed them at our work.

By the end of the summer I was beginning to wonder what next. I went to see my doctor; I thought of trying to get in at the children's hospital. He told me that although he was sure I should be able to do the work, no doctor would pass me, as I still had an irregular heart beat. I began looking in the evening paper again, and saw an advertisement for a sewing hand at Jowett Motors. Mr Dixon let me have time off to go and apply. I was told they wanted someone to work a power machine, for sewing

Bandstand, Lister Park, about 1914
(Photo courtesy of Bradford Libraries)

the linings for the upholstery in the cars. I said I was used to the machine, though I had only used one when testing them at Singer's shop. I got the job, to start the following week. I was one of about eight machinists. The car linings were mostly of flannel or rexine. Making them was not particularly difficult; the main thing was that the stitching should be straight. Making the roofs for the open tourers was quite a different matter, and made your arms ache, twisting and turning the rexine around. We were on piece work and usually earned about 27s. a week. I walked to work along with another girl who lived nearby; it was about two miles, mostly uphill. We enjoyed those walks, but we could have eaten a good breakfast when we arrived. We started at 8 a.m., and worked till 12, when we had an hour for lunch. There were no tea breaks in those days. There was no canteen either, so we had sandwiches and ate them by our machines. Then we would sit outside or go for a short walk. We got on well together, and I didn't dislike the work, but I did dislike the noise. We worked on a kind of landing above the workshop floor, and could look down and see the men banging and hammering away at the different parts of the motors. I continued working at Jowett's for nearly two years. Then I got involved in a dispute over wages and conditions, and was asked to leave.

My eldest sister emigrated to Australia in 1927. She had friends out there. I missed her quite a lot, as like me she was fond of swimming and we often went to the baths together. She sailed on Christmas Eve. My brother Charlie and I went to see her off at Tilbury. We went to London on the night train, then on to Tilbury in the early hours of the morning, only to be disappointed: the fog was so thick we couldn't see the liner, and after seeing her onto a boat that was taking the passengers out, we turned round and came home. One day soon afterwards, I was going down to the labour exchange to sign on, and was thinking of Bella and our swimming jaunts. She had always taken swimming very seriously and had said she was going to try to get work on the baths. That gave me an idea: why not go down and see if there were any vacancies? After all I had a qualification, the bronze medallion of the R.L.S.S. No sooner thought about than done. I called at the Windsor Baths and asked to see the Superintendent. I had to wait a while. Then I was received into his office, and I asked if there were any vacancies. He took particulars and then said, "Well, as a matter of fact, we do want an assistant on the slipper baths at Oswald Street, can you start on Monday?" I replied that I could, and so started my career as a swimming teacher.

I went to Oswald Street and reported to the other lady there, Mrs Jones, who was in charge. She booked the customers in and attended the four

"I worked at the open air baths in Lister Park, later known as the Lido."
(Source: City of Bradford *Open-Air Swimming Bath, Lister Park.*
Official Opening, 19th June 1915. Brochure)

baths downstairs; I attended the six upstairs. The men on their side did the same and attended to the boiler. We were kept busy, especially at week-ends. Very few working-class homes had bathrooms; most people bathed in a tin bath in front of the fire. But on Friday nights as soon as the mills closed we would be full of workers waiting for a bath. The price was 4d., and it saved all the messing about, heating water, and clearing the bath away at home. Saturday morning was always busy; indeed we were often busy right up to closing time at 8 p.m. We worked a 52-hour week. The wages was 32s., which was very good in those days.

The following summer I was sent to Drummond Road baths to attend the swimming. Drummond Road, where I had run for a shower years ago, and where I had done most of my swimming. I enjoyed the work. It was tiring and noisy, but at the end of the day I could go in for a swim, and no charge. Saturdays were the busiest time, as everything had to be left clean over the week-end. The cubicles, the wooden foot boards, and the bath side, all had to be washed. We had one Saturday afternoon off in three weeks, and a day off a week. Besides being a bath attendant, I was to give instruction in swimming to anyone who bought an instruction

Maggie sweeping up leaves at the Lido, Manningham Park.
(Photo courtesy of James Ogden)

ticket. This was quite interesting work, because you met people and chatted with them.

The next two summers I worked at the open air baths in Lister Park, later known as the Lido. It was very pleasant there when the weather was fine, though of course that only made us busier. There were more regulations to enforce then than later. Mixed bathing was very new, and something that had to be carefully watched. The dressing boxes on the right-hand side were for males, and on the left-hand side for females. They each had their own footbath. Men must only get in or dive from their own side, and ladies from their side. They had separate diving boards. They must only get out on their own sides. Hence if they wanted to have a little talk they sat at one end or the other. In fact about all the time they were mixed was when they were in the water. Bathing costumes, which were not so revealing as they are now, were not to be loosened. When the young men got out to dress, they would slip their shoulder straps down, and bare their manly chests, in order to have a good rub, before going into their cubicles. One day an Alderman, one of the Baths Committee, paid a call, and saw a young man drying himself

QUEEN'S HALL.
VIEW LOOKING TOWARDS KING'S HALL.

"When the open air baths closed for the winter months our services were required
in the King's and Queen's dancing halls, as cleaners and cloakroom attendants."
(Source: City of Bradford. *The Windsor, Bradford. Souvenir* 1919)

with his costume down to the waist. The Alderman just bawled in a voice
like thunder, "Put that costume up!" The young man looked round
wondering what all the noise was about, until an attendant went and
pointed out what was the matter.

When the open air baths closed for the winter months our services
were required in the King's and Queen's dancing halls, as cleaners and
cloakroom attendants. I rather liked cloakroom duty; it was pleasant to
hear the music and watch the dancers. The two chief orchestras were
Arthur Jackson's and Stanley North's. The dances usually finished at
1 a.m., and we were brought home by taxi. We still worked a 52-
hour week; we were allowed time off during the day to cover our time on
cloakroom duty. There was no overtime or extra payment for "unsocial
hours".

After a few years on the baths I was given a teaching round, spending
days at different baths. I was responsible for the safety of the swimmers
and sometimes teaching. The children from the schools came down for

One of the author's life-saving classes about 1950.
(Photo courtesy of Margaret Walter)

instruction, and I really liked teaching them. It was most rewarding to
hear a child of ten shout, "I can do it, I can swim!" I also taught swimming to various clubs which came to the baths after closing time. I was
paid extra by the clubs, so I was doing quite well financially. As a regular
member of staff I paid superannuation and had a sense of security; I would
not be dismissed except for serious misdemeanour. I realised I had a good
job. I determined to improve my swimming, and in time took all the exam-
inations of the R.L.S.S., gaining their Diploma in 1934. I took the A.S.A.
Elementary and Advanced Teachers' Certificates in 1935. Before I was
married I spent most of my time at the baths.

Looking back, I think the late nineteen-twenties were wonderful years
for the young. There was a great seeking for physical fitness; games
were the thing, and were coming within reach of the working class. Swimming was always my first love, but in Manningham Park you could have a
game of tennis or putting, or a row on the lake, for a few pence. This was
the great time for rambling clubs. They would meet in groups of twenty to
thirty, take the bus or tram out of town, and tramp the moors around. We
had a club connected with the Sunday School, but it usually met on a
Saturday, so I was unable to go. Sometimes a few of us would go after
class on Sunday, often walking across the moors to Ilkley and coming

back by bus or train. We enjoyed the wonderful views and the peace of the countryside. We always called walking *rambling*, a much nicer and more descriptive word, I think, than *hiking*, which came along later. Cycling clubs were also prominent, and every Sunday morning saw them setting off for the open roads, riding in twos, heads down. Winter evenings were spent at home, with occasionally a visit to the music hall. We held dances at Sunday School, and raved about the Charleston and the Black Bottom. Most of my friends were married, but I had no great longing to join them in that happy state. I did miss my old friend Eva Beecroft when she got married and went to live at Leeds. She always had such a lot to talk about and was so interested in social affairs; we did try to put the world right. We had what was called "the flappers' vote": every woman over twenty-one was entitled to vote. We were glad when Margaret Bondfield was appointed Minister of Labour, the first woman to hold a Cabinet post. We thought the Lloyd George health scheme a great help, enabling working people to draw a few shillings a week when off sick.

By the nineteen-thirties things were not so good. In my own family, my eldest brother George was unable to get work; he had met a young woman and wanted to get married, but as things were, the prospect was hopeless. Alice had married, and her husband was out of work. Even casual labour was hard to get; for every job there were fifty applicants. There were great queues outside the labour exchanges, and the few shillings the men received hardly kept them in food. They became discontented. Some who had fought in France for a shilling a day came home to poverty: was this the land fit for heroes to live in? Women too were restless, and whenever they could get a job they took it, and the men stayed and looked after the home; no longer was it a stigma on the man if his wife went out to work, but it was not a happy state. Most families thought themselves lucky if they had one member working. Wages were low, however, because labour was so easy to obtain. Unions tried to get the workers amalgamated in order to stop the reduction in wages.

I remember coming home one lunchtime, and seeing a line of sandwich board men parading down Darley Street. I thought how cold and tired they looked, traipsing the street that cold winter day. Then I noticed one of them grinning at me. It was George. He with a few others had been sent from the labour exchange to advertise a sale at one of the large stores. A week's work: what did it matter if the iron bars cut into your shoulders and your feet were numb? I think George must have done every kind of labouring job, until he managed with the help of his old army officer Captain Heseltine to get a regular job in the mill. He also got married.

It was about this time that the "means test" was brought out. Anyone who had been drawing unemployment benefit for a certain number of weeks was sent to a work centre, where he was set to saw logs. Each week he was there, his card was stamped, and when he had got the requisite number of stamps he could again draw unemployment benefit. An official also came round to his home, to see what possessions he had, and if any of them could be sold. All the wages of any other members of the family were enquired into, and the number of people living in the home was noted. At the end of these enquiries he was probably told that there was sufficient coming into his house to keep him, and that was that. Fathers were made to feel dependent on their children, brothers that they were being supported by their sisters, and everyone that they were living at rock bottom. There was only one way the young men who could not get work could force an ungrateful country to redeem in part the pledge of homes fit for heroes to live in. They left home, went to sleep in some disused attic let by a neighbour or a friend for a shilling a week, and then applied for assistance, saying that their family had thrown them out until they had got work. They were then given the assistance which was denied them as long as they remained at home. It was a sorry state of affairs and one that the Government seemed unable to cope with.

My own family life was not so grim. One of our great interests at this time was in Amy Johnson and her flight to Australia; a truly remarkable achievement, and made by a Yorkshire lass, as we never tired of telling ourselves. Radio was now beginning to creep into the home; first the earphones, then the radio set. The piano and gramophone were pushed out, which was a great pity. We used to have good times on winter evenings round the piano, and the gramophone had long been a favourite with us. We had records of "The Desert Song", "In a Persian Market", and of course all the popular songs of the day. I joined the Banjo, Mandolin and Guitar Club. I played the mandolin. We used to practise once a week or more, at a club or in one another's houses. We gave performances at Sunday School concerts and garden parties. We entered for the Grand Rally of Banjo, Mandolin and Guitar Clubs, British Federation, Northern Section, and played in the Tower Ballroom, Blackpool, in 1932. There were ten bands competing, and we came fourth. The following year with nine bands competing we came seventh, but we had a great time. It was about this time that the first "talkie" film was shown in Bradford, at the Savoy Theatre in Darley Street, since pulled down. We discussed this at some length. It was wonderful to hear the voice of Al Jolson singing "Sonny Boy", but quite a lot of us thought the talkies would spoil the cinema. We had grown up with the silent films. However, we had to give in to progress, and we gradually found ourselves enjoying the talkies, and wondering how we had found the silent films so entertaining.

Chapter 12

Married Life

The year 1933 saw some big changes in my life. In January my father, who had been on the pension for about three years, was taken ill and died suddenly. In April George got married, and in July Lilian. Now only mother, Charlie and myself were at home. All the family except Bella lived round about and came home regularly, so we were not short of visitors. But it was now I met my future husband, Stanley Newbery.

Stan worked for his brother, Walter, who had started a small garage in Valley Parade. Our friendship began like a lot more, by chatting as we met in the street. As he had a motor bike he invited me to ride pillion. I enjoyed this, and it wasn't long before he was taking me to Ilkley, Bolton Abbey, and the Yorkshire dales. He worked very late, often up to 10 p.m., as they were trying to build the business up. I often taught at the swimming clubs in the evenings, so we didn't spend a lot of time together during the week. Our longer trips were mostly taken on Sundays and holidays. But he usually came and met me from work, and on the nights that I finished at 8 o'clock we would sometimes go for a ride round. Our favourite run was to Heaton and Stoney Ridge, where you got such a lovely view of the Aire valley. It was here one evening when we were watching the sunset that he asked me to marry him. I had no hesitation in saying yes; we were in love, and I knew I should never meet a kinder or more thoughtful man. Stan had been through the First World War and had seen such misery and suffering that all he now wished to do was to bring a little happiness into the lives of all he came in contact with. He was five years older than I, and I was thirty-two. We agreed to wait a while, and to save up, so that we could begin our lives together without any debts.

Later this year we removed to 30 Ashbourne Drive, off Bolton Road. The old house in South Parade seemed too big now. My mother grieved for father, and I too missed him very much. Charlie, who worked on the railways, was transferred to Rotherham, and came home only at the week-ends, so during the week my mother and I were alone at home. The new house was just a small semi, on what was then a new estate, but with a nice position and a garden back and front. We were soon busy decorating, and planning the garden. I know my mother enjoyed living at Ashbourne; she took an interest in the garden, and we were blessed with good neighbours. She looked forward to visits from my sisters: Bessie and Annie now both had three children, and Alice had two. In due course Lillian and her husband moved to a house nearby. I enjoyed living at Ashbourne too; it was more airy and pleasant than South Parade, but we missed the spaciousness of the old house, and we had so many happy memories of it.

While we were courting Stan and I spent the first of many holidays at my aunt and uncle's farm at Out Newton, in the Holderness district of East Yorkshire. We went by train, and my aunt met us with the trap at Withernsea station. We arrived about 8 p.m. just as the daylight was fading on a cold wet night. We climbed into the trap and pulled our coats more warmly about us, covering our knees with an old rug. My aunt had one or two calls to make. Then we set off along the coast road at a gentle trot, my aunt pointing out anything of interest. Now the rain was coming down steadily, and a mist was gathering over the sea, what she called a sea roak. She didn't seem at all disconcerted by the rain, but was quite happy to jog along talking all the while, often to the horse, Daisy, who was very moody, and would only trot if she wanted to. Eventually we arrived, and found a good warm fire burning in the kitchen grate. We were all wet and cold, and thankful for the hot tea we were soon drinking. I know Stan thought the joys of riding in a trap were greatly overrated; but he grew to love the farm and the district. The farmhouse was a pleasant, rambling old building. Most of the village of Out Newton had disappeared into the sea; there were only five farms and two cottages at this time. Farming was still a precarious way of earning a living, but during the 1939-45 war the Government realised that they must help farmers with subsidies if we were to survive, and then farming really began to pay.

I had lived up at Ashbourne for three years when Stan and I decided to get married. Like all young folks we had our problems. I knew that I should lose my job on getting married, married women at that time not being employed by Bradford Corporation, and Stan's wage as a mechanic was less than mine. But we had saved enough to put down a deposit on a house, and we were fortunate in getting a small terrace house on Cornwall Road, near where Stan worked; so back I went to the district where I had spent the greater part of my life. The house consisted of five rooms: kitchen, with a fireside cooking range; front room, used at week-ends and sometimes in the evening; two bedrooms; and an overall attic. There was a keeping cellar and a coal cellar. The kitchen was our dining and living room; we also had a bath put in, with a table top over it. Bathing

The wedding of Maggie and Stanley Newbery, 1937
(Photo courtesy of Margaret Walter)

was really a pleasure; you stepped out of the bath in front of a lovely coal fire.

We fixed our wedding for 26 June 1937, and it was to have been at 10.30 a.m., but the parson was a cricket enthusiast who wanted to go and watch Yorkshire, so we altered the time to 10 o'clock, much to the annoyance of my sisters, who had to get their young families ready and get across to the church so early. But you can't please everyone; and when Stan realised Yorkshire were playing I was afraid he was going to offer to go with the parson. The marriage took place at Salem Church, Oak Lane, and we had the reception in the schoolroom. There were about 40 guests, mostly family, with a few friends. After the reception we set off on our honeymoon; we had now acquired a small car, an Austin 7, and we felt very fine as we set off. We had a few days in the Lake District, staying at Thirlspot. It was glorious weather and we enjoyed tramping around.

When I came home and started housekeeping I felt quite lost. There wasn't enough work to keep me busy. I was interested in cooking, but I soon found that £2 a week didn't go far, and I was glad to ask my mother about the cheaper cuts of meat and how to make the money spin out. We paid the building society 25s. a month; electric and rates took 10s. a week, and coal 4s. That left £1 for food and clothes. My purse was always empty at the week-end. Then Stan got a rise of 5s. a week, which certainly helped a bit. We were able to run the car, because that was in with the job, and Stan was allowed two gallons of petrol a week. He also got tips now and again. We were both determined not to get into debt, so as our parents had done before us we just did without the things we could not afford. Pictures and the theatre were something to be saved up for and managed about twice a year. I often wished I could go out to work, and I did take one or two little jobs helping people, but these only lasted a week or two. I missed the life at the baths. I missed meeting people and especially the teaching. I would walk across to my mother's two or three times a week, calling on Stan's father as I went.

One morning when I was feeling rather depressed, wishing there was something I could do, I had a visitor from the Bradford Education Department, who asked if I was interested in teaching swimming one half-day a week. The teaching of school children had now been taken over by the education department and was no longer done by members of the baths staff. Of course I was overjoyed. I was to be paid 9s. 6d. for a morning's work, which consisted of four classes of three-quarters of an hour each. They were all primary classes, of children between nine and eleven years of age. I went along to Manchester Road baths the following week. They were all big classes, of 40 or over. However, we got on well, and the teachers who brought the children were very helpful. Manchester Road baths was very suitable for teaching, not too deep, with a nice broad surround, onto which the dressing boxes opened, so the class was under your supervision all the time. We soon had a group of swimmers who could be safely left in the deep end to practise the tests set for them. Another group was in the four foot area, where they could practise a few strokes under the supervision of the teacher. The largest group was at the shallow end, where I worked most of the time, teaching them to help each other to gain confidence, and finally to try by themselves. Any swimming aids were frowned on in those days but I did have a rubber ring which I lent to any very timorous child. Most children love the water and at that age are very eager to learn. I enjoyed the work, and the money certainly came in very useful. We managed to put some away in the bank; there was no Welfare State in those days, so we were saving for a rainy day or for old age.

We were now in 1938. Rumours of Hitler's activities were much discussed and were very disquieting, but we tried to convince ourselves that there simply could not be another war. Too many of us remembered the last one. Then on 3 September 1939 we were again at war with Germany. All the talks had availed nothing. Though we were confident that it would soon be over, there was not the singing and the glory about this war that there had been about the 1914-1918 one. We remembered the train loads of invalids coming back from the front, and those who did not come back. We were all issued with gas masks and told it was an offence not to wear one when the sirens went to indicate an air-raid. We were to carry them with us wherever we went. Then all the windows had to be blacked out, not a glimmer showing. A.R.P. (Air Raid Precaution) units were formed. Men who, because of their age or physical disability, were unable to join the forces, joined the A.R.P. and became very thorough at their job of spotting a chink of light. During the winter months, when it was very dark, we were allowed to use torches, but they had to be turned to the ground. If you went out without one, you followed anyone that had one and happened to be going your way. Sometimes it became like a game of follow-my-leader, with quite a string of torchless persons behind. This was fine as long as the leader knew the way, but if he missed it, which was quite easily done, he was then faced with a group of tired and exasperated people, all having different ideas of which way to go, and cursing Hitler and all his kind.

The baths were taken over as decontamination centres, so all swimming was temporarily suspended. I lost my morning's work, but shortly afterwards I was advised to be ready to go with some of the children who were going to be evacuated. This came as quite a shock, but you just didn't argue in those days. When Stan came home from work we talked it over, and decided it was best to get the old haversack out and get it packed. The following morning I went to the school where the teachers were busy marshalling the children. I asked the headmaster if he needed me, and he said, "Just help us down to the station, and then you can go home — we have plenty of staff to deal with the billeting at the other end". We walked down Manchester Road, all talking and laughing; the children mostly looked upon this as a holiday. Having seen them on the train I went home, unpacked my haversack, and got Stan's tea ready.

Provisions soon became scarce in the shops, with queues forming, but this time the Government was quick to bring in rationing, which did give a fair deal to all, though it was very little. At one time it was ten pennyworth of meat each for the week, two ounces of butter, and two ounces of margarine or lard. It was amazing how we made it spin out. Every drop of fat off the meat was saved, in order to get enough dripping to eke out the butter ration. Bone broth became the order of the day, and very nice it was too, if you could get a nice shin bone. All luxuries seemed to disappear, except on the black market. Most people thought they were lucky if they knew a farmer, and got a few eggs or a bit of pork when a pig was killed on the quiet; this was considered "fair game", as we say in Yorkshire. But a new group sprang up among us, the spivs. These people disliked work, but seemed to get on very well, by selling on the black market anything that was scarce, at an exorbitant price. Food was their chief commodity, but they would sell anything, and if it wasn't what it was represented to be, well, you had no redress. They adopted a style and posture of their own, wearing coats with lots of padding in the shoulders to add to their width. They usually walked with a hunched, slouching gait, and tried to give the impression that they were very knowing. To be designated a spiv was not at all complimentary, and this title was soon given to all the layabouts. The spivs were also known as "the wide boys".

Talking of the black market reminds me of a time when we had a chance of a piece of pork. This sounded wonderful after living on little bits of stewing meat, liver, and bone broth. My husband came home and said a friend of a friend of his, who had a farm, was going to kill a pig for Christmas. Would we like some? We would have to take a big piece and divide it among our friends; the man wanted rid of it as soon as possible. We agreed to have a piece, and the following night Stan brought it home, a side of pork. Then it was a case of where to put it. We decided on the cellar, till the next night, when we would cut it up and get it delivered to our friends. But the next afternoon I was going out to the shops and stopped to have a word with my neighbour. She said, "I wonder what that man's after? He's calling at every house, and looks like an official of some sort or other". I watched him come out of one house and go into the next. He was in about seven minutes. He was still a long way off. My guilty conscience flew to the side of pork: what if they were searching for it? I went back to the house. Where to hide it? It seemed to stick out a mile. At last I dumped it behind one of the easy chairs in the sitting room and went out again. My neighbour was still there. She said, "He's about four doors away". I replied that I couldn't wait any longer, as I must get into town and back before tea, and went off. When I returned I called next door to see if the man had been. "Yes. He was one of those evacuee officers, and he wanted to know what accommodation you had, so as to assess how many evacuees you could take. He went into every room, sizing it up and making an entry in his book. I told him your house was just the same as mine, so he isn't going to bother calling back on you". This was a relief. That evening we cut the pork up and delivered it. The following day we had pork for dinner. It was good, but I said to Stan, "Don't bring any more black market goods home - my nerves won't stand it!"

In the war years the chief topic of conversation seemed to be food, and where to get something different. We were exhorted to eat more potatoes; they suddenly acquired great nutritional value. We were unable to get rice, but could obtain Soyagetti as a substitute; it was quite nice but very starchy. Home baking almost ceased, as it was impossible to get all the ingredients. Recipes for cakes without eggs were popular; I still have two which I use occasionally, a chocolate cake and a fruit loaf. I also remember a great deal of time was spent on "make do and mend". Nothing was discarded until it was virtually in ribbons. We made mittens out of the tops of men's socks. When the foot of the sock was past repairing, it was cut off just above the ankle; by stitching round, the welt became the welt of the mitten, and the leg the mitten. At least it kept the hands warm. Clothing coupons were always scarce; we never got enough, hence all this contriving to save a few where we could.

It was about August 1941 when I had a visit from Miss Hardaker of the Education Committee, to ask if I would be prepared to take an evening class of swimmers. They had started a Youth Club at St Mary Magdalene's schoolroom, and one of its activities was to be swimming, using the baths at Green Lane School, which was quite near. Of course I was again delighted to get back to work. My hours were 7–9 p.m., and I received 9s. 6d. a week. The following Monday night (girls' night) I reported to the club and found I had over sixty children to teach. The bath was only small, 50 feet by 15, and with so many children attending the numbers had to be limited. They were divided into three groups of about twenty, and each group had a swim and a lesson for about half an hour. I encouraged them to practise for the life-saving awards, and the last half hour was always given over to this. There were other activities across at the club: a games room, two billiard tables, two table tennis tables, a reading room, and a buffet. The age limit was 14 to 21. The club was started with poor children of the district in mind. It was a great boon because there was so little for young folks to do during those early war years. The children loved it. And we were blessed with some dedicated and tireless workers: Mr Dawson, the headmaster at Green Lane; Mr Rodley, from Grange Grammar School; Mr Proctor from

Drummond Road School; and Miss Wann. Mr Dawson left us after a few years and Mr Rodley took his place as Youth Leader. I stayed for 25 years, and Mr Rodley retired about three years after me. We lived to see some of the children of our first members become members, and to see some of the tearaways and hoodlums become decent-minded young men and women. And we enjoyed our work.

I had not been long at the club when I had a month off. Our daughter Margaret was born in January 1942. This was a great event. However we were able to fit things in so that I could go back to the club. Stan was doing firewatching two nights a week as his war effort, but he was able to be exempt on Mondays. Later I took a second youth club swimming class on Wednesday evenings. This was from the Stella Maris Youth Club; the members came from the other side of town to Green Lane baths, and often had to walk, but they were keen to swim. I enjoyed these classes, the extra money was welcome, and Stan did not mind being the babysitter, as he was content to sit and listen to the radio or read a book. With a young child I found my days more fully occupied. I believed in getting out as much as possible, and often took Margaret in Manningham Park or across to my mother's. It was a pleasant walk up Bolton Lane in those days. There was a stream, the banks of which were covered with Monkey Musk, a bright orange flower that looked lovely in the sun. Now the stream has been piped and neat little semi-detached houses with neat little gardens have sprung up on either side of the road. It is still a nice road, but not the country lane it used to be.

Soon Margaret was out of her pram and running around with the other children in the neighbourhood. She was always a lively child and brought us a great deal of joy. We always thought the rations were inadequate for growing children. It seems funny now to think of how we went around looking for something tasty for tea. Once when Margaret was about three years old, we went round the market in town and asked at several stalls if they had any potted meat or polony, and always got the same answer: no. We finally called at the building society to pay the monthly premium. Margaret piped up as we reached the counter, "Have you any polony?" This caused a laugh amongst the queue, but I still went home without anything for tea.

We still had the car, and although petrol was rationed we usually managed to go for a short run at the week-end. Ilkley, Bolton Abbey, and Blubberhouses were our favourite runs. We also visited friends and relations. Stan's brother and his family lived at Skipton; we visited them occasionally and had several holidays there. We usually went at Whitsuntide. They were chapel folks, and always took part in the Whit

Walk. This was a big event; all the churches and chapels joined in a procession round the town, each with their own banner. It finished in front of the Town Hall, with hymns and a prayer. Our chapel then usually went to a playing field, and held races, followed of course by tea and buns. On some of the snaps taken at these feasts we look rather old-fashioned; but a very enjoyable time was had by all. These were the days when you sought your own entertainment with your own family, friends, and neighbours.

The war went on, and we began to wonder if we should ever know peace again. We were fortunate in having only two air raids over Bradford, but we felt for the other towns, London and Coventry especially, that bore the brunt of it all. We listened to J. B. Priestley's Sunday night broadcasts, and received a lot of encouragement from them. I always thought J. B. Priestley had a lovely speaking voice, and whatever the fortunes of war were, he remained calm and gave confidence. We heard on the radio about the siege of Stalingrad, and admired the courage of the Russians as they held on to their city. Our privations were nothing to what these people, and indeed the German soldiers, must have suffered during the Russian winter. Eventually the news from the front took a better turn, and at last came that glorious day when peace was declared. We were not as excited as we had been in 1918. We were older. No doubt the young ones were just as excited as we had been. Fires were lit in the streets again, and in some streets tables were brought out and a tea put on for the children. We took Margaret to the tea on Lupton Street, and stayed a while, talking with neighbours.

We soon found out that although the war was over it was going to be some time before things got back to normal. Indeed rationing continued for a long time. There was not quite as much hardship and confusion as there had been in 1918. The men were released from service more slowly. Men who had no work to go to were sent to training centres to learn a trade. They were thus absorbed into industry more steadily but there was still a lot of unemployment. It was some time before the baths were open to the public again. Some of them needed a lot of repairs and alterations. There must have been a great number of children passing through school in the war years and immediately after who never had the chance to learn to swim at school. It was not till 1947 that Miss Hardaker again visited me and asked if I could take two half-days' swimming, one at Drummond Road, where I had the children from Whetley Lane School, one at Wibsey, where I had those from St. Joseph's. Margaret was now five years old and attending Green Lane School, but there was no problem, as she went to her father at the garage till I called for her.

We continued to enjoy simple pleasures. Our evenings would be spent listening to the radio or entertaining a few friends. We rarely went to the theatre or pictures. On Saturdays in winter Stan watched the football matches at Valley Parade. At Christmas we had family parties with carol singing and games of Blind Man's Buff, Hunt the Thimble, and of course Putting on the Donkey's Tail, which always caused a lot of fun. We usually had our Skipton relatives over for a day round about this time, when we went to the pantomime at the Alhambra. In the winter we seemed to spend a great deal of time shovelling snow, or watching Margaret and the other children sledge down Cornwall Road, as we had done ourselves years ago. On Sundays in summer, after Margaret had been to Sunday School, we would have a run to the dales. We used to love to go round the abbeys: Fountains, Jervaulx, Rievaulx, and Byland. The old monks knew how to choose sites for their abbeys; they always set them in beautiful surroundings. We never got tired of these places, and motoring was a pleasure in those days. The roads were not as good as they are now, but they were not so crowded, and you could go along in a very leisurely way. We would often stop to watch the cricket at Beckwithshaw; I think watching cricket is an ideal way to spend Sunday afternoon. We continued to visit relatives and friends, especially my sister Hetty, as Stan and her husband seemed to have a lot in common. They were both keen on sports and could talk cricket and football by the hour. Then there was my friend Eva and her husband Jack. We had our holidays at Out Newton, spending long afternoons with Margaret and her cousins, swimming and paddling from the quiet beach there. We were content. I don't think we would have had life much different, and there were thousands more living in much the same way.

In February 1949 we had a party for my mother's eightieth birthday. It was held in Commerce House, Bradford, where my sister Alice and her husband were the caretakers. This was quite an occasion. There were six daughters, three sons, ten grandchildren and two great-grandchildren; and with all the in-laws there were thirty-eight members of the family present. A few weeks later mother was taken ill, and she died on 13 April. We consoled ourselves with the thought that at least she had been spared a long illness, and remembered mother had always said she hoped we would not grieve for her. We were all pleased to think that the last years of her life had been reasonably comfortable. She had been a great reader, and was seldom without a library book. She used to love a game of cards, or "Sorry", a card game that was popular about 1940 but seems to have gone out of fashion. Her life had not been easy, but I never heard her moan, and she certainly had a great capacity for making the best of

"In February 1949 we had a party for my mother's eightieth birthday"
Back row, left to right: Charlie, Lillian, Maggie, Hetty, Harry
Front row, left to right: Annie, Bessie, Mother, George, Alice
(Photo courtesy of Margaret Walter)

things. I would say that, especially in the last years of her life, she had great contentment. Until you lose your parents, you don't realise what a hold they have on the family. We were all used to going home at least once a week, when we heard the family news, and often met each other. We certainly missed mother greatly, and I think as a family we drifted apart a little.

Chapter 13

Never So Good?

The war still lingered with us. Identity cards were not abolished till 1951. It was 1953 before all rationing was ended and you were able to buy whatever you wished, providing of course that you could pay for it. Stan's wages had risen and I had my part-time work, so although prices were going up we were able to get a few luxuries. Now we were entering the "you've never had it so good" era.

Things were changing in the educational world. At the age of ten, children were preparing for the "11-plus" examination, which went a long way to determine their future. If they passed, they went to a Grammar School, where if they adapted themselves to their studies they could, by gaining the required number of "O-levels", go into the VIth Form and take their "A-levels", and if the passes were good enough they could obtain a grant to cover the initial cost at a University. This was really marvellous; the sons and daughters of working-class parents could by their own diligence get the education that had always been the prerogative of the rich. It was something the Labour Party had long worked for, and it was grand to see your children get the benefit of these reforms and not have to turn out at 6 o'clock to go to the mill as we had done. Bessie's boy went to Grammar School and eventually obtained a managerial post in the electrical industry. Annie's boy also went to Grammar School and became an accountant. Hetty's two boys went on to University; it was not easy for Hetty and Bill financially, but they managed, and their joy was in their family. Margaret went to Grammar School but decided to leave at sixteen and went to work in the civil service. All the children had received a better education than we had done, even as we had received a better education than our parents.

Now we started looking for a house with a garden, and eventually we got one on the Ashbourne estate, not far from where my mother had lived. There was a living room (or "lounge" as they are now always called), a kitchen with a pantry and store cupboard, two small bedrooms and one large one, and a bathroom with an inside toilet. This was very nice, as going across the yard to the toilet on a winter's night was really most unpleasant. The house needed decorating throughout. We worked in the evenings stripping and papering the walls. We had help from family and friends, and got it into shape before moving in on 3 August 1957. My husband wanted a garage before the winter, and we had to clear the drive and level the site; eventually the garage was delivered and erected. Then Stan got all the back garden turned over ready to sow the vegetables the following Spring.

In September there was an outbreak of flu. Margaret took it first. She was very ill with it, and before she had fully recovered I went down with it. We were in a bit of a pickle as we hardly knew our neighbours, but we managed with a little help, and then learnt that almost all the neighbourhood had been afflicted, people leaving their keys outside so that their doctors could call. Stan developed pneumonia. He was very ill for a few weeks, and then the doctor told me that he would never be able to do his own work again. Stan had suffered with a weak chest ever since leaving the army, and the flu had caught him just when he was run down. The doctor said he would probably be able to do light work later on, but light work is hard to get when you are 62 years old. This was indeed a blow. However, we did not tell Stan just then. We decided to carry on as usual as far as possible. Margaret had just left school and started work with the Inland Revenue. I of course had my part-time work, which I could get back to as soon as Stan was well enough to be left.

I explained our situation to Mr Averis, the Director of Physical Training for Bradford, and said I would be pleased to do any extra work, and would preferably like to work full time. He was most sympathetic and promised to do all he could to have me put on the full-time staff. I had now been employed by Bradford Education Committee in a part-time capacity for 18 years, and before that by the Corporation Baths full-time for 10 years. But I was now 57 years old, and that was the snag; I was judged too old to be put on the staff. They allowed me to work full time on a part-time basis, and I did so for about eighteen months. Then the powers-that-be said if I worked full time I must be put on the staff; but, argued the other powers, this woman is too old to be put on the staff. The outcome was that I worked four-and-a-half days instead of five, thus proving myself a part-timer and making everybody happy.

Soon it was Christmas. I particularly remember the Youth Club Party that year. As usual we had a pea and pie supper. We had a few guessing games before supper; then the pies were brought in all hot and steaming. Great big pies these, as big as would cover the floor of a large oven. They were cut into portions and served with the peas. No tinned peas these, but peas that had soaked all day and then cooked slowly with a ham bone; the result was lovely. After supper more games, then dancing. We had a pop group to play for this. I was astounded when the dancing started, to see the gyrations of the young folk. My mind went back to the gay twenties when the Charleston was in vogue, but this was even more fantastic. The young men picked their partners up and threw them around like trained athletes, and though the perspiration streamed down their faces they yelled for more. Their dancing was absolutely uninhibited, and they enjoyed every minute of it. I think it was Tommy Steele who popularised rock and roll. It was a great time for the young ones, but I was old enough to realise it was not for me. I would rather have a nice slow waltz.

Stan recovered from his illness sufficiently to drive the car, so he was able to take Margaret and me to work, thus saving us the waiting for buses. But he suffered from asthma, and there were days when he just couldn't go out. That was when we found the television a great joy; it was grand to be able to follow cricket, tennis, and golf on the screen, and also to get the news. Stan also did odd jobs around the house.

It was a good thing that we had now gone all-electric. We had an electric washing machine. True, we still had to put the washing through the ringer, but we didn't have to turn it; the ringer went by electricity. Gone were the days of scrubbing, boiling, possing, and mangling. Then we had an electric oven, automatic, that you could set to the desired temperature; no more guesswork as to whether the oven was hot enough for the Yorkshire puddings. Yet it was surprising how you got used to coal ovens and could tell by putting your hand in if one was hot enough for what you wanted. The greatest advantage of the electric oven seemed to me to be the cleanliness. It had been such a sooty business cleaning the coal oven flues: one at the top from which the soot had to be scraped onto a shovel, one at the side which you did with a flue brush, and then one at the bottom. Then there was the job of getting the soot into the dustbin without it blowing back into your face; I managed by wrapping the shovel in a newspaper. I was glad to be done with these chores. We had been living at Ashbourne about two years when we decided to have an electric fire in the lounge. I remember the first electric fires I ever saw, about fifteen years earlier, at Christopher Pratt's on North Parade. It was a cold night and they had a window display of them, electrical fires with coal effects. They looked so warm and cosy, but the prices were absolutely prohibitive and I never thought I should possess one. We got one with the fire effect, and how easy it was now to get the fire on in the morning!

Stan accepted the fact that he would not be able to go to work again, but was determined to do as much as he was able. We got a small greenhouse, which was a great pleasure to him, and we had quite good crops of tomatoes. We still had our runs in the car, and we had quite a few trips to Crayke and Kirk Hammerton, to see the farms where I had lived as a child. These places were really flourishing, and in a much better state of repair than they had been. But as his illness got worse Stan had to spend periods in hospital, including a fortnight at Middleton Hospital near Ilkley, when he seemed to make progress. The doctors there were very kind, as was our own doctor, Dr Minchom, who told us not to hesitate to ring any time day or night. Sometimes when he was at home Stan would have an attack during the night, and I would get up and run to the phone box to get Dr Minchom, who always came immediately and gave an injection which eased the pain; and sometimes the following day he would be quite well again, and would be out in the garden. I gave up my work in order to attend to him. On his good days we would have short runs to the moors. My sister Hetty, who had been a widow two years, also loved the moors and was always ready to join us.

In January 1965 Margaret got married. Her husband, Donald, left school after taking his A-Levels and had worked in industry for eighteen months, but had now been accepted at London University to study medicine. They went to live at Carshalton in Surrey, and how we missed Margaret! At Whitsuntide 1966 they came up as usual for the holidays. Margaret was expecting her first child and we were all very happy. Then Stan was taken ill again and entered Bradford Royal Infirmary. He had been in and out of hospital so many times that I think I didn't quite realise that inevitably there must be a last time. Pastor Evans from Sunbridge Road Mission was a frequent visitor, and I realised afterwards that he had tried to prepare me for the end. Stan died on 1 June 1966. We had all visited him in the afternoon. During the night he had an attack from which he never recovered. He didn't live long enough to see his grand-daughter Jenny, who was born the following September.

We had twenty-nine years of happy married life; surely this was something to be thankful for. Margaret and Donald stayed with me a while but eventually went home. What a blank there is when your partner has gone; it seems so futile to go on doing things. I tried to interest myself in the garden, but I soon grew tired. Then I would go visiting, especially to see Hetty; we would have walks together, or sit in the garden. There was Eva too, who had also lost her husband; we would chat over old times. But there was still a lot of time to fill in, and I decided to go and see if there was any part-time work at the baths. I was given one half-day a week, and soon got another. This gave me an interest and helped the pension along - I was now 66 years of age and an Old Age Pensioner, but I was very fit and able to cope with the work without any distress.

Margaret and Donald now had a house in Sutton, Surrey, and I went down to see them about four times a year. I was there when their second daughter, Sheila, was born in 1969. I now found myself listening to the more affected accents of the Southerners and often hearing Yorkshire folks referred to as only half-civilised. They had to concede that we could and did raise cricketers. I did however meet some very kind people and was made very welcome at West Street Mission, the chapel Margaret and Donald attended. I took advantage of my visits to see a bit more of London, and while London with all its pomp and tradition is not for me, I can understand the Londoners' love of it. And of course there is always something going on.

In September 1970, when Donald had completed his course at London University and gained his B.Sc. with Honours, he looked for a place to do research, and finally gained one with Dr Eccleston's Brain Metabolism Unit at Edinburgh University. I was pleased, as it was the kind of work he wanted. I imagined myself taking trips to Scotland now instead of London. Then Donald came to see me and suggested I should join them up in Scotland; he would get a house big enough to allow me to have my own rooms, and thus retain my independence, while I should be at hand for babysitting and, as he put it, for Margaret to keep an eye on me, as she worried about me being alone. Well, I didn't take long to make up my mind. It seemed to me that I could live a more useful kind of life with them, so in November 1970 I left Bradford and came to live in Edinburgh. Margaret and Donald had got a large terrace house in Lee Crescent, Portobello. I helped them with the decorating; we had got the house in order before Margaret's third baby, Kathryn, arrived on 26 March 1971. I have a large lounge with a room divider screening the kitchenette, and a small bedroom. The lounge is on the first floor and has a large bay window. It faces south-west, so we get a lot of sun, which makes the room very pleasant.

I certainly missed my sisters and friends that first year here. I had to get used to a new way of life, which is not easy when, as we say in Yorkshire, you are top side of sixty. We all went to the Baptist Church, where we met some very friendly people. The Minister and his wife, Mr and Mrs Gellaitry, came and chatted to us and made us welcome. It was difficult at first to understand their language; as Jenny once said, "Why do these people talk like this?" I suppose it was just as difficult for them to understand us. We have now been here three years and Jenny and Sheila have both acquired a Scotch accent. Jenny has been going to school two years, and Sheila starts soon. Kathryn is now a lively two year old, and there is another baby, Louise. Four girls who keep Margaret and Donald busy, and bring a great deal of pleasure to all of us.

I have joined a dressmaking class, not because I am particularly fond of sewing, but for the company. I have made myself a very nice dress and skirt. I went to the corner shop for some pins one day and was asked 10p for a small box. I thought of Rendalls' shop in Kirkgate, Bradford, where when I was a girl you could buy anything in the haberdashery trade. Almost everything was marked down to something and elevenpence three-farthings, and in lieu of the farthing change they would give you a paper of pins, 100 pins. I never saw a shop window with so many different articles displayed in it as theirs; I have spent hours looking in that window.

Well, I have certainly seen a lot of changes in the last seventy years, and no doubt there will be as many in the next seventy. I think perhaps children change least of all. This summer my two grandchildren went on their Sunday School Trip. I went with them. A bus was hired and we boarded her at 10 a.m. The children were all given streamers, which they fixed in the windows and much to their delight saw blown about as the bus proceeded. They sang songs, but there was no one to hear them; the roar of the traffic drowned their voices. When they arrived at Spylow Park they straightaway started to run over the field, climbing the bank, and generally enjoying themselves. The lunch arrived in a van, and a huge tarpaulin was spread on the ground nearby. Bags of food were served out to each child, far too much; a huge minced beef pie, a packet of crisps, an iced bun, and chocolate biscuits. Oh, the whoops of delight as the children brought these goodies forth! I am afraid a lot of it was wasted. The healthy twelve and thirteen-year-olds made short work of it, but the little ones gave a lot to the birds. Orange juice was served in disposable cups. After lunch the sweet van arrived, and those who had some money could stuff themselves still further. They enjoyed every minute of it. They played their own games. Skipping ropes came out, and the chants began:

> Polly in the kitchen, doing some stitching,
> In came a bogey man and pushed Polly out.

> Little fat doctor, how's your wife?
> Very well thankyou, that's allright:
> Can't eat a bit of fish, nor a stick of licorice,
> O.U.T. spells out!

And so they went on. Races were held for the different age groups, the same old wheelbarrow and sack races that we had run years ago. With an egg-and-spoon race for mothers; this caused a lot of fun. When everyone was tired out, tea was served. The packets were handed out again; this time instead of the mince pie there was a sausage roll. Again a lot of waste. After tea the men and boys settled down to a game of cricket. Most of the girls just sat and watched. Others wandered off for a walk or in search of wild flowers. The young ones played ring games, went on the swings, or just ran around. About 6 p.m. the bus came. The field had been cleared of litter, by the offer of a prize from Mr Gellaitry for the boy or girl who collected the most. Everyone piled into the bus again, saying what an enjoyable day they had had. Streamers were given out again and were soon floating out. Another Sunday School Treat was over, but may there be many more.

I think perhaps the greatest change in the last fifty years is in women's and children's dress. I feel hot at the thought of all the clothes we wore as children. There was first a cotton chemise, reaching down to your bottom. This was usually gathered into a band at the top, so the garment itself was very full. Over this you had a bodice, or comforter as they were usually called. Then drawers which came down to your knee. Over these in winter would be flannel and cotton petticoats; in summer the flannel one would be discarded. Then a thick cloth dress for the winter and a cotton one for summer. You always wore pinafores to keep your dresses clean; these were usually white calico, but often made out of the best parts of old shirts. Wool stockings worn with heavy boots completed your outfit. The boys wore suits, with the trousers coming into a band just below the knee and fastening with a button. They also wore white rubber collars that had to be washed every day; these were starched so that they stood upright. When they had been worn a while they became frayed at the edges and chafed the neck. Most of the boys took them off or untied them as soon as school was over. My brothers were always losing theirs. How much freer and more comfortable are the children of today in their tee-shirts and short trousers, and the girls in their pretty nylon dresses! The ladies' dresses are much more comfortable too, and of course people have many more dresses than they used to do. In the days when you took your material to the dressmaker, it was made to last, and not discarded till it was threadbare; even then the good parts were cut out for patching or for making clothes for the children.

Now it is 1973 and we are living in the affluent age, so they tell us. And things certainly have improved. There is Social Security, which prevents the dire poverty of sixty years ago. I don't know whether people are happier. Happiness comes from people themselves, and especially by making others happy. Now much of our excitement comes from watching the television. A few weeks ago the greatest talking point was the Sky Lab Project, when three astronauts spent twenty-eight days in space and were brought back and landed safely. This week the main topic is cricket. England are in a very sticky position in the third test against the West Indies, and will need a Wilfred Rhodes to get them out of this. I am now up to the present, so it is time to leave the past and look to the future. It is 11.25 a.m., just time to get the telly on and see how England are making out.

Chapter 14

Conclusion

It is now 1979, and quite a lot has happened since I wrote the last chapter. Donald finished his studies and took a post with a firm at Hull. Neither he nor Margaret wished to live there. They looked for a house in Beverley, and eventually got one with a lovely big garden which they thought would be delightful for the children, and so it has proved. The house has four bedrooms, and I had the small one, along with a room downstairs. I was quite happy; I could identify myself with Beverley. My parents had talked of these parts and we had relatives here. I still liked the town; I didn't think it had changed since I used to spend my holidays here with Grandma and my aunt. We all settled in nicely, and during the holidays we found time to have a few trips to Hornsea and Bridlington. We certainly were a bit crowded at home, so I looked for a little cottage and got one.